Best of JAMAICA

BEST OF JAMAICA

JAMAICA AT 60

The Gleaner Company (Media) Limited

A member of the RJRGLEANER Communications Group

IMPACTING JAMAICA

First published in Jamaica in 2023 by
The Gleaner Company (Media) Limited
7 North Street, Kingston

ISBN: 978-976-612-020-7 (hbk)

A catalogue record for this book is available from the National Library of Jamaica

Cover and Book Design by Christina Moore Fuller – Krissbiskit Kreative

Printed and Bound in China

contents

Ackowledgement vii

Introduction: What is Right with Jamaica ix
His Excellency The Most Honourable Sir Patrick Allen ON, GCMG, CD, KST.J, Governor-General ix

1960s
Cultural Beginnings • 1962 1
End of an Era • 1962 3
Jamaica Celebrates Independence • 1962 4
Introduction to Television • 1963 7
'Miss Jamaica' Wins Miss World Title • 1963 8
Air Jamaica Inaugural Flight • 1966 9
Jamaica Stock Exchange Opened • 1969 10

Put Fun an Joke Aside!
Fae Ellington 12

Resilience is in Our DNA
Christopher Zacca 15

Best of Jamaica – 60 Years On
Dennis Chung 17

Flow ... A Proud and Steadfast Partner in Jamaica's Development 20

1970s
Manufacturing Boom • 1970 23
Foreman vs Frasier Boxing Showdown • 1973 24
Minimum Wage • 1975 25
Cindy Breakspeare Wins Miss World Title • 1976 26
Bob Marley Peace Concert • 1978 27

Born in Jamaica: A Symbol of Caribbean Pride
Minna Israel 28

Resilience: The Source of Our Greatness
Patrick Hylton 30

JAMAICA 60 – To the World and Beyond!
Sanjay Lewis 32

Rooted in Resilience and Boldness – JNCB 34

1980s
Montego Bay Becomes a City • 1981 37
HEART Trust Launched • 1982 38
Jamaica Bobsled Team • 1988 39

Every Cloud Has a Silver Lining
Dr Neil Gardner 40

The Urban Development Corporation
Dianna Blake-Bennett 42

Wi Likkle but Wi Tallawah!
Nicola Madden-Greig, OD 44

The Mico University College 46

1990s
Lisa is Miss World • 1993 ... 50
Jody-Ann Maxwell Wins Scripps Howard Spelling Bee • 1998 ... 51
Reggae Boyz Qualify for France World Cup • 1998 ... 52

'Wi Likkle but Wi Tallawah':
An Indomitable Spirit to Honour at Jamaica Sixty
Joey Issa ... 53

Tribute to Trelawny Yellow Yam
M.A. Stewart-Hinchcliffe ... 55

The People: The Spirit and Continued Show of Resilience of The People Of Jamaica
Chris Williams ... 58

Supreme Ventures: Interwoven into the Very Fabric of Jamaica ... 60

2000s
Emancipation Park Opens in Blaze of Lights and Music • 2002 ... 65
Queen Elizabeth II Visits Jamaica • 2002 ... 66
Portia Simpson Miller Sworn in as First Female PM • 2006 ... 68
Portmore Toll Opens • 2006 ... 70
Jamaica at the Beijing Oympics • 2008 ... 71

The Indomitable Spirit of the Jamaican Woman
Senator Janice S. Allen ... 76

Commitment to Country
Peter Melhado ... 78

Out Of Many, One
Sheila Benjamin ... 80

2010s
Jamaica Celebrates 50 Years of Independence • 2012 ... 83
London Olympics • 2012 ... 85
Moscow World Champs • 2013 ... 88
Barack Obama Visits Jamaica • 2015 ... 91
JSE on Top of the World • 2015 ... 94
Reggae Boyz Reach Gold Cup Final • 2015 ... 95
General Election • 2016 ... 96
Jamaica at the Rio Olympics • 2016 ... 98
Jamaica's First Female Prime Minister Bids Goodbye • 2017 ... 101
First Female President of Methodist Church • 2018 ... 102
Reggae Girlz Qualify for Women's World Cup • 2018 ... 103
Toni-Ann Tops the World • 2019 ... 104

The Finest of Lines
Gary 'Butch' Hendrickson ... 106

Empowerment of Oracabessa – In Harmony with Nature
Thalia Lyn ... 108

2020s
Koffee Toast of Grammys • 2020 ... 111
Several Women Sworn in as Parliamentarians • 2020 ... 112
Commodore Antonette Wemyss-Gorman Takes the Reins • 2021 ... 113
Elaine Thompson's Triple Gold Feat at the Tokyo Olympics • 2021 ... 115
First Woman Pastor at Baldwin Episcopal Church • 2021 ... 117
William and Kate's Royal Visit • 2022 ... 118
JAMAICA celebrates 60 years of Independence, A DIAMOND JUBILEE • 2022 ... 121

ACKOWLEDGEMENT

WE THANK YOU ...

Sixty years after Jamaica's political independence, you hold in your hands a book that captures some of the Best of Jamaica.

Thanks to the many persons from across multiple sectors, including Jamaica's Governor-General His Excellence the Right Hon. Sir Patrick Allen, who shared their views of what they regard as positive aspects of the country. This publication would not have been possible without your support. We salute you.

To the team in the Information Systems Department of the Gleaner Company (Media) Limited for their diligent research to pull some of the most inspiring stories about Jamaica for inclusion in this book. We salute the team of Sheree Rhoden (Department Manager), Andre Cunningham, Ahon Gray and Karel Townsend.

We thank too editor and proofreader Paul Williams and project supervisor Garfield Grandison, a former Editor-in-Chief and General Manager of the Gleaner Company (Media) Limited.

In this souvenir publication you are introduced to some of the things that represent the best of Jamaica – individuals, institutions, places and things that make the country a good place to live, work and raise families. It will show too the importance of not ignoring what's right with Jamaica despite the challenges we face as a nation.

Let's celebrate Jamaica!

What is Right With Jamaica!

His Excellency The Most Honourable
Sir Patrick Allen ON, GCMG, CD, KST.J
Governor-General

It is difficult to imagine any country on Earth that has not been touched by a Jamaican. In my travels, I have seen the impact of our people's ideas, food, businesses, music, sports and other contributions in countries around the globe. From Asia to South America, Europe to Africa, the South Pacific and Australia, North America and throughout the Caribbean, we are a people who 'season the pot' wherever we go.

The colourful *patois* (Jamaican Creole) and our distinctive personalities attract and intrigue many individuals. We are special, unique, and greatly admired. We are not a perfect people, however, we can use what is right with Jamaica to fix what is wrong. That is the message and the mandate we must inculcate as we continue to build a solid foundation for the future.

What is fundamentally right with Jamaica is our stable democracy which has allowed us to transfer power successfully from one political party to another without any coups for the past 60 years. We have respected, embraced and faithfully followed our strong constitution.

With much urgency, we have to heighten attention to the education of our children as they are our most valuable assets. Solomon, 'the wisest man' who ever lived, advised us, *"Start children off on the way they should go, and even when they are old, they will not turn from it."* We need to be careful with how we grow the next generation of citizens, for it is by our example that they can leave indelible footprints at home and on the global community.

In this 60th year of our Independence, we cannot hide behind mistakes of societal ills or count failure as an option. We have seen challenges that seek to break, divide and damage the fibre of who we are as Jamaicans. However, we were not, and will not be destroyed, because we are resilient.

Anyone in Jamaica, despite race, colour, creed, religion, or economic situation, can rise, and as National Hero The Right Excellent Marcus Garvey said, "*We can accomplish what we will.*" Our history beckons us from within the dark conflicts of the past to be steadfast and leave a legacy of hope. We have overcome much, and we will do so yet again, and again, and again!

It is of dire urgency that we reinforce our value system, which ensures that no one is deprived of his or her God-given right. We have no option but to love and care for our communities, build selfless relationships that will bind us together, respect and love one another unconditionally, exercise the duty of care, protect and keep our children safe, empower our youths to be productive citizens, support our farmers, and take care of the land that God has given to us.

As we work together to build a stronger and better Jamaica for the future, 'I believe' must be incorporated into the fabric of everything we do, so that we can demonstrate with confidence, "I believe in the destiny of Jamaica."

Excellence must be our watchword. For within the seemingly trivial tasks of our daily lives, we disclose our true character by which we will be evaluated. For this reason, our goal should always be, "*Only the best is good*

enough!" We have consistently resisted any notion that seeks to define us by our shortcomings, and we have chosen to elevate the many good things that characterise the glory of our nation.

We have made outstanding contributions to the visual and performing arts, culture, sports, education, tourism, medicine, research and development, science and technology, international relations, global peace initiatives, advocacy on behalf of developing countries, and human rights.

There have been instances of evolution and transformation as we strive to '*build a new Jamaica*'.

Now, as we stand at the crossroads of history, it is imperative that we equip ourselves to make the right choices in meeting the challenges that face us. We must zealously guard our ideals and embrace the task we have been given to improve this great nation.

I still believe, "*There is nothing wrong with Jamaica that cannot be fixed by what is right with Jamaica.*" Those sentiments echoed from my heart when I accepted the honour of serving this nation as governor-general and they still fuel the optimism that I have for Jamaica.

As you read this publication, which highlights and documents the nation's accomplishments, I trust you will be inspired to remember that the best of Jamaica is yet to be discovered, because the best of Jamaica lies in the heart of every Jamaican.

I urge everyone to follow the imperative of Marcus Garvey and "*lose not courage, lose not hope, go forward ... 'Re-igniting a nation' ... to be the best of ourselves.*"

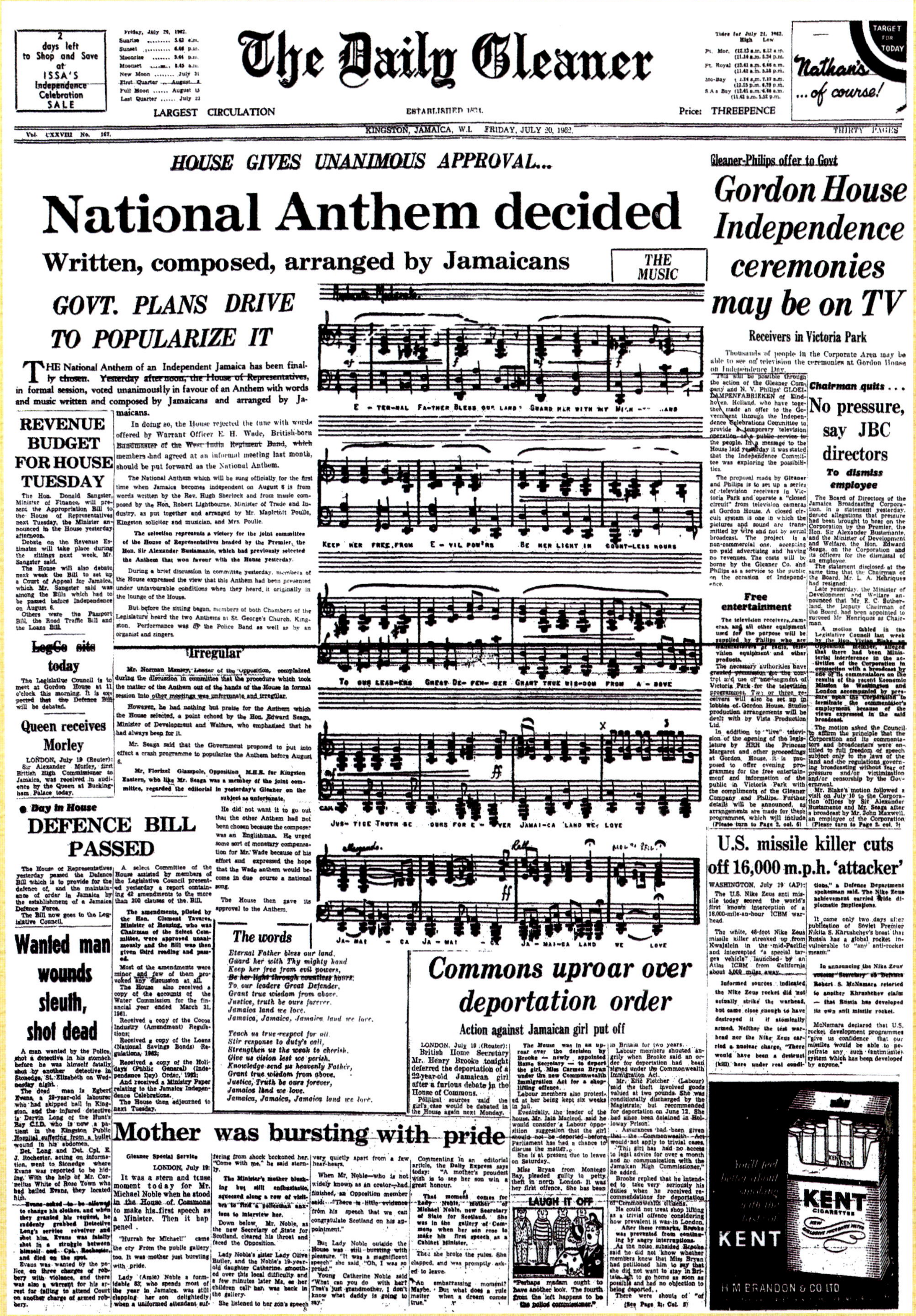

2 days left to Shop and Save at ISSA'S Independence Celebration SALE

Friday, July 20, 1962.
Sunrise .... 5.42 a.m.
Sunset .... 6.46 p.m.
Moonrise .... 3.44 p.m.
Moonset .... 3.45 a.m.
New Moon .... July 31
First Quarter .... August 8
Full Moon ...... August 15
Last Quarter ...... July 23

The Daily Gleaner

LARGEST CIRCULATION — ESTABLISHED 1834. — Price: THREEPENCE

Tides for July 21, 1962.

Nathan's ... of course! TARGET FOR TODAY

Vol. CXXVIII No. 167. — KINGSTON, JAMAICA, W.I. FRIDAY, JULY 20, 1962. — THIRTY PAGES

HOUSE GIVES UNANIMOUS APPROVAL...

National Anthem decided

Written, composed, arranged by Jamaicans

GOVT. PLANS DRIVE TO POPULARIZE IT

THE National Anthem of an Independent Jamaica has been finally chosen. Yesterday afternoon, the House of Representatives, in formal session, voted unanimously in favour of an Anthem with words and music written and composed by Jamaicans and arranged by Jamaicans.

In doing so, the House rejected the tune with words offered by Warrant Officer E. H. Wade, British-born Bandmaster of the West India Regiment Band, which members had agreed at an informal meeting last month, should be put forward as the National Anthem.

The National Anthem which will be sung officially for the first time when Jamaica becomes independent on August 6 is from words written by the Rev. Hugh Sherlock and from music composed by the Hon. Robert Lightbourne, Minister of Trade and Industry, as put together and arranged by Mr. Mapletoft Poulle, Kingston solicitor and musician, and Mrs. Poulle.

The selection represents a victory for the joint committee of the House of Representatives headed by the Premier, the Hon. Sir Alexander Bustamante, which had previously selected the Anthem that won favour with the House yesterday.

During a brief discussion in committee yesterday, members of the House expressed the view that this Anthem had been presented under unfavourable conditions when they heard it originally in the lounge of the House.

But before the sitting began, members of both Chambers of the Legislature heard the two Anthems at St. George's Church, Kingston. Performance was by the Police Band as well as by an organist and singers.

'Irregular'

Mr. Norman Manley, Leader of the Opposition, complained during the discussion in committee that the procedure which took the matter of the Anthem out of the hands of the House in formal session into other meetings was unfortunate and irregular.

However, he had nothing but praise for the Anthem which the House selected, a point echoed by the Hon. Edward Seaga, Minister of Development and Welfare, who emphasised that he had always been for it.

Mr. Seaga said that the Government proposed to put into effect a crash programme to popularize the Anthem before August 6.

Mr. Florizel Glasspole, Opposition M.H.R. for Kingston Eastern, who like Mr. Seaga was a member of the joint committee, regarded the editorial in yesterday's Gleaner on the subject as unfortunate.

He did not want it to go out that the other Anthem had not been chosen because the composer was an Englishman. He urged some sort of monetary compensation for Mr. Wade because of his effort and expressed the hope that the Wade anthem would become in due course a national song.

The House then gave its approval to the Anthem.

THE MUSIC

The words

Eternal Father bless our land,
Guard her with Thy mighty hand
Keep her free from evil powers,
Be her light through countless hours.
To our leaders Great Defender,
Grant true wisdom from above.
Justice, truth be ours forever,
Jamaica land we love.
Jamaica, Jamaica, Jamaica land we love.

Teach us true respect for all,
Stir response to duty's call,
Strengthen us the weak to cherish,
Give us vision lest we perish.
Knowledge send us heavenly Father,
Grant true wisdom from above.
Justice, Truth be ours forever,
Jamaica land we love.
Jamaica, Jamaica, Jamaica land we love.

REVENUE BUDGET FOR HOUSE TUESDAY

The Hon. Donald Sangster, Minister of Finance, will present the Appropriation Bill to the House of Representatives next Tuesday, the Minister announced in the House yesterday afternoon.

Debate on the Revenue Estimates will take place during the sittings next week, Mr. Sangster said.

The House will also debate next week the Bill to set up a Court of Appeal for Jamaica, which Mr. Sangster said was among the Bills which had to be passed before Independence on August 6.

Others were the Passport Bill, the Road Traffic Bill and the Loans Bill.

LegCo sits today

The Legislative Council is to meet at Gordon House at 11 o'clock this morning. It is expected that the Defence Bill will be debated.

Queen receives Morley

LONDON, July 19 (Reuter): Sir Alexander Morley, first British High Commissioner to Jamaica, was received in audience by the Queen at Buckingham Palace today.

● Day in House

DEFENCE BILL PASSED

The House of Representatives yesterday passed the Defence Bill which is to provide for the defence of, and the maintainance of order in Jamaica by the establishment of a Jamaica Defence Force.

The Bill now goes to the Legislative Council.

A select Committee of the House assisted by members of the Legislative Council presented yesterday a report containing 42 amendments to the more than 200 clauses of the Bill.

The amendments, piloted by the Hon. Clement Tavares, Minister of Housing, who was Chairman of the Select Committee, were approved unanimously and the Bill was then given third reading and passed.

Most of the amendments were minor and few of them provoked any discussion at all.

The House also received a copy of the accounts of the Water Commission for the financial year ended March 31, 1961.

Received a copy of the Cocoa Industry (Amendment) Regulations;

Received a copy of the Loans (National Savings Bonds) Regulations, 1962;

Received a copy of the Holidays (Public General) (Independence Day) Order, 1962;

And received a Ministry Paper relating to the Jamaica Independence Celebrations.

The House then adjourned to next Tuesday.

Wanted man wounds sleuth, shot dead

A man wanted by the Police, shot a detective in his stomach before he was himself fatally shot by another detective in Stonedge, St. Elizabeth on Wednesday night.

The dead man is Egbert Evans, a 29-year-old labourer who had skipped bail in Kingston, and the injured detective is Dervin Long of the Hunt's Bay C.I.D. who is now a patient in the Kingston Public Hospital suffering from a bullet wound in his abdomen.

Det. Long and Det. Cpl. E. J. Rochester, acting on information, went to Stonedge where Evans was reported to be hiding. With the help of Mr. Cornelius White of Rose Town who had bailed Evans, they located him.

Evans asked to be allowed to change his clothes, and when they granted his request, he suddenly grabbed Detective Long's service revolver and shot him. Evans was fatally shot in a struggle between himself and Cpl. Rochester, and died on the spot.

Evans was wanted by the police, on three charges of robbery with violence, and there was also a warrant for his arrest for failing to attend Court on another charge of armed robbery.

Gleaner-Philips offer to Govt

Gordon House Independence ceremonies may be on TV

Receivers in Victoria Park

Thousands of people in the Corporate Area may be able to see on television the ceremonies at Gordon House on Independence Day.

This will be possible through the action of the Gleaner Company and N. V. Philips' GLOEILAMPENFABRIEKEN of Eindhoven, Holland, who have together made an offer to the Government through the Independence Celebrations Committee to provide a temporary television operation as a public service to the people. In a message to the House laid yesterday it was stated that the Independence Committee was exploring the possibilities.

The proposal made by Gleaner and Philips is to set up a series of television receivers in Victoria Park and operate a "closed circuit" from television cameras at Gordon House. A closed circuit system is one in which the pictures and sound are transmitted by wire and not by aerial broadcast. The project is a non-commercial one, accepting no paid advertising and having no revenues. The costs will be borne by the Gleaner Co. and Philips as a service to the public on the occasion of Independence.

Free entertainment

The television receivers, cameras, and all other equipment used for the purpose will be supplied by Philips who are manufacturers of radio, television equipment and other products.

The necessary authorities have granted permission for the control and use of one segment of Victoria Park for the television programmes. Two or three receivers will also be set up in lobbies of Gordon House. Studio production arrangements will be dealt with by Vista Production Ltd.

In addition to "live" television of the opening of the legislature by HRH the Princess Margaret and other proceedings at Gordon House, it is proposed to offer evening programmes for the free entertainment and information of the public in Victoria Park with the compliments of the Gleaner Company and Philips. Further details will be announced, as arrangements are made for these programmes, which will include

(Please turn to Page 2, col. 6)

Chairman quits . . .

No pressure, say JBC directors

To dismiss employee

The Board of Directors of the Jamaica Broadcasting Corporation, in a statement yesterday, denied allegations that pressure had been brought to bear on the Corporation by the Premier, the Hon. Sir Alexander Bustamante, and the Minister of Development and Welfare, the Hon. Edward Seaga, on the Corporation and its officers for the dismissal of an employee.

The statement disclosed at the same time that the Chairman of the Board, Mr. L. A. Henriques had resigned.

Late yesterday, the Minister of Development and Welfare announced that Mr. E. C. Sutherland, the Deputy Chairman of the Board, had been appointed to succeed Mr Henriques as Chairman.

A motion tabled in the Legislative Council last week by the Hon. Vivian Blake, an Opposition member, alleged that there had been Ministerial interference in the activities of the Corporation in connection with a broadcast by one of its commentators on the results of the recent Economic Mission to Washington and London accompanied by pressure upon the Corporation to terminate the commentator's employment because of the views expressed in the said broadcast.

The motion asked the Council to affirm the principle that the Corporation and its commentators and broadcasters were entitled to full freedom of speech subject only to the laws of the land and the regulations governing broadcasting without fear of pressure and/or victimization and/or censorship by the Government.

Mr. Blake's motion followed a visit on July 10 to the Corporation offices by Sir Alexander Bustamante and Mr. Seaga after a broadcast by Mr. John Maxwell, an employee of the Corporation

(Please turn to Page 2, col. 7)

U.S. missile killer cuts off 16,000 m.p.h. 'attacker'

WASHINGTON, July 19 (AP): The U.S. Nike Zeus anti missile today scored the world's first known interception of a 16,000-mile-an-hour ICBM warhead.

The white, 48-foot Nike Zeus missile killer streaked up from Kwajalein in the mid-Pacific and intercepted "a special target vehicle" launched by an Atlas ICBM from California about 5,000 miles away.

Informed sources indicated the Nike Zeus rocket did not actually strike the warhead, but came close enough to have destroyed it if atomically armed. Neither the test warhead nor the Nike Zeus carried a nuclear charge. "There would have been a destruct (kill) here under real conditions," a Defence Department spokesman said. The Nike Zeus achievement carried wide diplomatic implications.

It came only two days after publication of Soviet Premier Nikita S. Khrushchev's boast that Russia has a global rocket invulnerable to "any anti-rocket means."

In announcing the Nike Zeus success Secretary of Defence Robert S. McNamara referred to another Khrushchev claim — that Russia has developed its own anti missile rocket.

McNamara declared that U.S. rocket development programmes "give us confidence that our missiles would be able to penetrate any such (antimissile) system which has been developed by anyone."

Commons uproar over deportation order

Action against Jamaican girl put off

LONDON, July 19 (Reuter): British Home Secretary Mr. Henry Brooke tonight deferred the deportation of a 22-year-old Jamaican girl after a furious debate in the House of Commons.

Political sources said the girl's case would be debated in the House again next Monday.

The House was in an uproar over the decision by Brooke — newly appointed Home Secretary — to deport the girl, Miss Carmen Bryan under the new Commonwealth Immigration Act for a shoplifting offence.

Labour members also protested at her being kept six weeks in jail.

Eventually, the leader of the house, Mr. Iain Macleod, said he would consider a Labour opposition suggestion that the girl should not be deported before Parliament has had a chance to discuss the matter.

She is at present due to leave on Saturday.

Miss Bryan from Montego Bay, pleaded guilty to petty theft in north London. It was her first offence. She has been in Britain for two years.

Labour members shouted angrily when Brooke said an order for deportation had been signed under the Commonwealth Immigration Act.

Mr. Eric Fletcher (Labour) said the theft involved goods valued at two pounds. She was conditionally discharged by the Magistrate, but recommended for deportation on June 12. She had since been detained in Holloway Prison.

Assurances had been given that the Commonwealth Act would not apply to trivial cases. "This girl has had no access to legal advice for over a month and no communication with the Jamaican High Commissioner," he added.

Brooke replied that he intended to take very seriously his duties when he received recommendations for deportation of Commonwealth citizens.

He could not treat shop lifting as a trivial offence considering how prevalent it was in London.

After these remarks, Brooke was prevented from continuing by angry interruptions.

As the noise subsided Brooke said he did not know whether members knew that Miss Bryan had petitioned him to say that she did not want to stay in Britain but to go home as soon as possible and had no objection to being deported.

There were shouts of "of

(See Page 2, Col. 5)

Mother was bursting with pride

Gleaner Special Service

LONDON, July 19: It was a stern and tense moment today for Mr. Michael Noble when he stood in the House of Commons to make his first speech as a Minister. Then it happened.

"Hurrah for Michael!" came the cry from the public gallery too. It was mother just bursting with pride.

Lady (Amie) Noble a formidable 83, who spends most of the year in Jamaica, was still clapping her son delightedly when a uniformed attendant suffering from shock beckoned her. "Come with me," he said sternly.

The Minister's mother blushing but still enthusiastic, squeezed along a row of visitors to find a policeman anxious to interview her.

Down below, Mr. Noble, as the new Secretary of State for Scotland, cleared his throat and faced the Opposition.

Lady Noble's sister Lady Olive Butler, and the Noble's 19-year-old daughter Catherine, smoothed over this local difficulty and a few minutes later Ma, as her children call her, was back in the gallery.

She listened to her son's speech very quietly apart from a few hear-hears.

When Mr. Noble—who is not widely known as an orator—had finished, an Opposition member said: "There is little evidence from his speech that we can congratulate Scotland on his appointment."

But Lady Noble outside the House was still bursting with pleasure. "It was a magnificent speech" she said. "Oh, I was so proud."

Young Catherine Noble said "What can you do with her? That's just grandmother. I don't know what daddy is going to say."

Commenting in an editorial article, the Daily Express says today: "A mother's proudest wish is to see her son win a great honour.

That moment comes for Lady Noble, mother of Michael Noble, new Secretary of State for Scotland. She was in the gallery of Commons when her son rose to make his first speech as a Cabinet Minister.

Then she broke the rules. She clapped, and was promptly asked to leave.

"An embarrassing moment? Maybe. But what does a rule matter when a dream comes true."

LAUGH IT OFF

"Perhaps madam ought to have another look. The fourth from the left happens to be the police commissioner."

KENT

H M BRANDON & CO LTD

The National Anthem for Independent Jamaica was chosen on July 19, 1962

1962

Rex Nettleford (left) in performance with fellow dancer Yvonne DaCosta at the Little Theatre in 1962.

THE DAILY GLEANER, WEDNESDAY, SEPTEMBER 19, 1962.

National Dance Company formed

JAMAICA now has a national dance company. It was announced yesterday by Messrs. Rex Nettleford and Eddy Thomas, two of our leading choreographers and dancers, that the National Dance Theatre Company of Jamaica has been formed, with a nucleus of the 15 best male and female dancers from the major dance groups of Jamaica.

They will work together now to bring to the public regular performances of works based on the many legends and folk lore customs which abound in Jamaica.

According to the spokesman for the group, dance, as an art form in Jamaica, is now sufficiently developed to be the means of projecting the movement patterns and customs of the island to people locally and abroad.

Thus, the National Company will maintain constant research and documentation of our folk legends and customs to be used as thematic material for new dances. It is planned to have a presentation at least once each quarter. Package shows will be taken around the countryside and field trips and demonstration lectures will be held.

The programme of the National Dance Theatre Company will be a two-fold one, half Jamaican and half modern creative.

Members of the company are required to take a minimum of three classes a week in modern and folk techniques as well as ballet. Facilities for the latter have been made available by Madame Soohih and the Rowe Sisters studios.

No auditions were held for the 15 members now in the Company, as they were chosen on repeated high standard of performance over the past ten years. New recruits will be added to the National Company, hereafter, by once-yearly auditions.

The dance in Jamaica

by REX NETTLEFORD

MR. NETTLEFORD — has been acting, dancing and directing shows from an early age in Montego Bay. As a member of the Ivy Baxter Group he danced important roles but always regarded himself primarily as a dance-creator. Since 1956 he has created dances in Jamaica, Trinidad, England and Ghana where he worked with very skilled theatre groups. Since 1959 he has been choreographing for the LTM pantomusicals and this year directed and choreographed the record-breaking "Banana Boy" for the LTM as well as co-devised the Independence dance show "Roots and Rhythms" for which he also choreographed the controversial "African Scenario". His real job is that of Staff Tutor in Political Education at the UWI.

A NATIONAL Dance Company of Jamaica has been formed and the Minister of Development and Welfare besides giving the new Company his blessings has decided to become a patron. This in a way marks off one phase of the dance movement which had its early beginnings some 15 years ago and now finds some fulfilment in the existence of some 15 or so active dancers of the highest calibre possible. It is a tribute to the dance and a challenge for Jamaica in the contribution it can make in this most expressive of the arts. But let us go back to the beginning...

Any emergent people with as varied a background as we have in Jamaica must sooner or later face the agony of choice. For we are many things besides being ourselves. We are mixtures of all the races of the world set in one place. We are at once a tonal complex of the melody of Europe played upon the rhythm of Africa.

And because we are set in the Americas, we of necessity come of late within the spiritual orbit of the American continents. With independence, the influences of Latin America and the North America are going to be even more telling.

It is relieving then that although Jamaican dancers have made certain choices, the search is not near ending. In fact it never ends. For Dance is the art of discovery. And while dancers are concerned with evolving a form "we can call our own", we have no intention of cutting ourselves off from the influences and techniques of older and more established idioms. There continues to be a place in Jamaica, therefore, for all the dance idioms.

The work of **Anatole Soohih**, carried on by his widow May Soohih, is evidence of this. And it is significant that one of the more important pioneers of the dance in Jamaica was classical ballet teacher, the late **Hazel Johnson**. Her contribution remains visible in the work of Faye Simpson, Barbara Fonseca and the Rowe sisters.

But probably most of all in the efforts of **Ivy Baxter**, the pioneer of the present dance movement. Miss Baxter's influence grows stronger daily all over the Jamaican countryside, largely through the Jamaica Social Welfare Commission's dance activities which she actually started and which is now carried on by Joyce Campbell, one of her past pupils.

Out of the early beginnings emerged people like Eddy Thomas and Clive Thompson who have both appeared on Broadway with the greatest of all modern dance companies —the Martha Graham Company; and there were early accomplished dancers like Cynthia Lee, Alma MockYen, Vilma Cupidon and Ronan Critchlow. The movement won the support of the UWI Extra-Mural Department which has invited tutors from the United States and Haiti for the past five years to conduct summer schools at the University. The contribution of Lew Smith of New York, Ferrick Darby and Neville Black, Jamaicans who studied in the States, and Lavinia Williams of Haiti has been positive.

Cultural exchange

Over the past two years, the author maintained in the absence of Baxter and Thomas the continuity in the movement placing emphasis on standards of excellence in performance and on dance-education.

For the first time dancers drawn from the different schools of dance worked together continuously and effectively together making it possible for a rich and varied national company to visit Baltimore and Washington D.C. in 1960 on a cultural exchange tour—a practice which it is hoped, will be developed in an independent Jamaica.

The celebrations in connection with Independence bore witness to the dynamism of the dance whether our dancers be in the villages, at the Denbigh Agricultural show, on the roadside concerts, in the musical—"Banana Boy" or in the Independence Dance Show "Roots and Rhythms."

With the return of Eddy Thomas from a Government of Jamaica Arts Bursary abroad, an added dimension is given the movement since Thomas is not only dancer and teacher but musician and designer as well. It is out of all this that has come the National Dance Theatre Company of Jamaica comprising some 15 dancers all of soloist calibre and drawn from such groups as the Ivy Baxter, the Soohih and Eddy Thomas schools of dance.

The dancers selected on the basis of strength of technique, performing capacity and ability and physical resilience to be the first members of the Company are:

Maureen Casserly—a dancer trained by Soohih and Thomas and who has shown remarkable versatility in roles she has created in both the classical and modern idioms.

Yvonne DaCosta — whose early classical training with Faye Simpson has provided a sound base for her efforts and skilled dancing both in modern and primitive roles.

Pansy Silvera—for years a principal dancer in the Faye Simpson Ballet School, has proven herself working with Thomas and myself as one of the most lyrical dancers in the Company.

Barbara Grant—a teacher at St Andrew High School who has studied in England is one of the most elegant and most vibrant of the female dancers in the Company and is also a versatile music-comedy actress-dancer as she has shown both in "The Boy Friend" and in LTM's "Banana Boy".

Monica McGowan — Who is well known for her sensitivity and dramatic power as seen in the role of Liza 'Eddy Thomas' "Legend of Lover's Leap". She runs a class for young dancers at the Half Way Tree Junior Centre.

Gertrude Sherwood — A dancer with an inborn power of projection. Miss Sherwood is a lab technician by profession but has proven herself to be a dancer with an excellent sense of co-ordination. She excelled as the African initiate in Nettleford's recent "African Scenario".

Joyce Campbell — At present acting dance officer to the Jamaica Social Welfare Commission, is known for her acting ability and was one of the leading exponents of many of Ivy Baxter's early works.

Shirley Campbell — A sister of Joyce's, is also not without her acting ability and is well known for her projection of wit, gaiety and vitality across the footlights.

Rosalie Markes—UWI science graduate has a power of expression which betrays an inner depth and power that has been used to its fullest in certain works in "Roots and Rhythms". She is married and with a growing family.

So is **Sheila Barnett** whose role as the sea-Nymph in the long ballet from the Mock-Yen—Thomas musical "Once Upon A Seaweed" is memorable. She projects a quality of dignity and nobility in everything she dances and is a dance teacher of considerable merits. Her interest is particularly in research and annotation of Jamaican dance movements.

Bridget Casserly—has emerged as a dancer with most pleasing lyrical quality which can be attributed to her early training at the Soohih Dance School.

Mavis Lai — Studied with Glen Gordon of the Rumsey-Gordon School and has a remarkable stage presence as well as the natural grace of many a Jamaican Chinese dancers.

Ronan Critchlow—A veteran dancer who emerged some years ago when he created the role of the Stowaway in Ivy Baxter's first full length ballet "Rat Passage". He is a civil servant and amateur painter but has recently returned from Antigua and Grenada where he taught dance and choreographed shows under the auspices of the Antigua Tourist Board and the Extra-Mural Department respectively. In Grenada he worked with the Bee Wee Ballet. He is also an excellent drummer and was responsible for drum scenes in many of Baxter's early work.

Audley Butler — Got his early experience in pantomime and then after "Busha Bluebeard" (1958 edition) joined up the Ivy Baxter Dance Group. A virile and quick-witted dancer Audley Butler has other attributes since he recently represented Jamaica at basketball in the 9th Central American and Caribbean Games.

Bertie Rose — a relative newcomer, has made remarkable strides as a dancer in the past three years. Since then he has tackled difficult leading roles with sensitivity and understanding and recently showed his skill at partnering in his pas de-deux with Joyce Clarke in the Rowe-Fonseca ballet "Tropical Delight", from the Independence Dance Show.

Eddy Thomas — co-directs the new Company. An excellent dance performer and teacher, Thomas was a 1959 Government of Jamaica Arts Awardee. He went to Martha Graham School and after many scholarships joined her Company to appear in the 1960 season on Broadway. He then appeared in "Kwamina" in which he worked with one of America's leading choreographers — Ahnes deMille. On hearing about the strides made in dance by dancers in Jamaica he decided to return to Jamaica expressly to start a National Company as well as to direct his Dance Workshop which he founded in 1958 after working for many years with Ivy Baxter. His contributions to "Roots and Rhythms" were among some of the best dance works ever exhibited in Jamaica including the Jamaica "Legend of Lover's Leap" and "Footnotes in Jazz". Mr. Thomas who has worked with many of the leading dance experts in America will help bring to Jamaica theatre a sense of finish and excellence which it needs to be of professional standard.

Other personnel of the Company will be announced later.

Members of the newly formed National Dance Theatre Company of Jamaica in October 1962. Front row: Eddy Thomas, one of the Directors, Bertie Rose, Audley Butler, Ronan Critchlow;

Middle Row: Shirley Campbell, Mavis Lai, Maureen Casserly, Bridget Casserly, Monica McGowan,

Back row: Sheila Barnett, Yvonne DaCosta, Barbara Grant and Pansy Silvera. Absent: Rosalie Markes, Joyce Campbell, Gertrude Sherwood and Rex Nettleford who was the other Director of the Company.

The NDTC was formed in 1962

The Daily Gleaner
LARGEST CIRCULATION — ESTABLISHED 1834 — Price: THREEPENCE
Vol. CXXVIII No. 279. KINGSTON, JAMAICA, SATURDAY, DECEMBER 1, 1962 TWENTY-SIX PAGES

An era ends as Sir Kenneth Blackburne goes

...GIVING WAY TO THE NEW

LAST BRITISH HEAD OF STATE DEPARTS — AFTER GUARD OF HONOUR INSPECTION AND SAD GOODBYES

Sir Clifford takes his place today

SIR KENNETH BLACKBURNE, Jamaica's first Governor General, accompanied by Lady Blackburne and their son Martin, yesterday waved a final farewell at Palisadoes Airport, boarded a BOAC jetliner and at 2.15 p.m. flew for London, on pre-retirement leave.

Big-2 will meet at private club

Mounts dais

Traffic jam

FINAL GOODBYES: Sir Kenneth Blackburne and Lady Blackburne (top) wave farewell to friends at Palisadoes Airport yesterday afternoon as they board a BOAC jetliner for New York en route to London.

Stadium the venue for swearing-in

Royal salute

SENATE SITS RECORD TIME

World Bank, IMF teams due next week

Jamaica's 2nd gold medal

This time from Colquhoun

COLQUHOUN (right) IN AN EARLIER FIGHT

Canada's High Commissioner

Crowd cheers Sir Winston

'Most grateful'

DEATH PENALTY

Resignation

OVERCROWDED SECONDARY SCHOOLS

Hundreds may never get in

See Sunday's Gleaner

UFCo team due tomorrow for talks on bananas

Some water rates up today

Idlewild crash kills 32

LAUGH IT OFF

"I only hope he'll be able to go back to worrying about business when this is all over."

End of an Era

1962

1962

Wednesday, August 8, 1962.
Sunrise ... 5.47 a.m.
Sunset ... 6.38 p.m.
Moonrise ... 12.19 p.m.
Moonset ... 12.06 p.m.
New Moon ... August 29
First Quarter ... August 8
Full Moon ... August 15

The Daily Gleaner

LARGEST CIRCULATION

ESTABLISHED 1834

Tides for Thursday, August 9, 1962.

Price: THREEPENCE

Vol. CXXVIII No. 186. KINGSTON, JAMAICA, W.I., WEDNESDAY, AUGUST 8, 1962 THIRTYTWO PAGES

JAMAICA CELEBRATES INDEPENDENCE

Princess opens first Parliament

HER ROYAL HIGHNESS the Princess Margaret at Gordon House, reads the Queen's Speech with which she declared open Jamaica's first Parliament, yesterday morning. On the dais with her are His Excellency the Governor General, Sir Kenneth Blackburne; the Earl of Snowdon the Princess' husband, and Lady Blackburne, with members of the Royal party among those standing behind. In front of the dais (at left) are the bewigged, Speaker of the House of Representatives, the Hon. Tacius Golding, and the President of the Senate, the Hon. Senator G. C. Campbell. In front of them are clerks of the Legislature, and at right, members of the Parliamentary Opposition.

...News received with satisfaction...' Khrush's telegram to Busta

MOSCOW, Aug 6 (Reuter): Mr. Khrushchev has sent a telegram to Sir Alexander Bustamante, Prime Minister of Jamaica, congratulating the people of Jamaica on achieving their independence, the Soviet news agency Tass reported tonight.

At the same time the Soviet Government has declared its recognition of Jamaica as an independent and sovereign state and has expressed its readiness to establish diplomatic relations with it, the agency said.

Mr. Khrushchev's telegram said: "Abiding by the great principles of equality and self-determination of the peoples, the Soviet Government has received with satisfaction news of the proclamation of the independence of the Jamaican people."

The all-union Central Council of Trade Unions has sent a telegram of greetings to the Jamaica trade unions in connection with the proclamation of the island's independence, Tass added.

"The Soviet working people heartily wish the working people of Jamaica big successes in the building up of a new life, in the struggle to raise the living standards, for democracy and peace" the telegram said.

From China

TOKYO Aug. 7 (AP): Both Nationalist and Communist China announced Sunday their recognition of Jamaica which becomes independent Monday.

President Chiang Kai-Shek, wired congratulations to Sir Kenneth Blackburne, then Governor of Jamaica and named Counsellor Yu Peng of the Nationalist Embassy in Lima, Peru, as special envoy to attend the Independence Day ceremonies.

Foreign Minister Chen Yi of

(Please turn to Page 2, col. 8)

Her Royal Highness in Throne speech:

UK and Jamaica wish to maintain bonds of friendship

THE FIRST PARLIAMENT of the independent Jamaica, summoned to a joint sitting by proclamation of Her Majesty the Queen, was opened in state at Gordon House yesterday morning by the Queen's sister, Her Royal Highness the Princess Margaret.

Before a full house of the newly-created Senators and of the Members of the House of Representatives and a glittering gathering of dignitaries from home and abroad, Princess Margaret read the Speech from the Throne in a clear and musical voice, and, with the assembly standing, read the Queen's personal message.

In her message, the Queen recalled her visit to Jamaica some years ago and added: "It is with every good wish for the future that I warmly welcome Jamaica to the Commonwealth Family of Nations."

Her Royal Highness entered the legislative chamber of Gordon House on the arm of her husband, the Earl of Snowdon and smiled to the legislators as she walked up the aisle to take her seat on the red-carpeted dais.

Multi-coloured

Her dress was of stiff white satin with the fitted bodice and the side panels of the bouffant skirt embellished in the embroidered crescent of diamonds, pearls and silver.

The royal gown gleamed with the medals of her orders and decorations, which included the blue sash of the Royal Victorian Order. Her tiara and necklace were pearls and diamonds.

In the distinguished visitors' gallery, the multi-coloured robes of delegates from Ghana and Nigeria, and the golden robe of the delegate from Ceylon contrasted sharply with the formal greys and blacks of the representatives of European powers and the United States and the Jamaicans and West Indians.

Seated nearest the Bar in the places of honour were Mr. Lyndon Johnson, Vice-President of the United States, and opposite him, Mr. Hugh Fraser, Minister of Aviation in the British Government and a former Colonial Affairs Under-secretary.

Said Princess Margaret to the assembled Parliament, on behalf of the Queen:

"My Government in the United Kingdom has laid down its responsibilities and has ceased to have any authority in and over Jamaica after more than 300 years of close association with the island and her people.

"But both my Government in the United Kingdom and my Government in Jamaica wish to maintain those bonds of friendship which have existed for over three centuries and have made it possible for Jamaica to proceed to independence peacefully and happily."

The Throne Speech added that

(Please turn to Page 2, col. 2)

Queen's message:

I warmly welcome Jamaica to Commonwealth

In a personal message to the Jamaican people read by Princess Margaret at the state opening of Parliament yesterday, Her Majesty the Queen said she was sure that Jamaica would have a vital contribution to make to the cause of fuller co-operation, understanding and tolerance far beyond the immediate area of the world in which the island is situated.

Text of the Queen's message follows:

"I have it in command of The Queen to read you the following message from Her Majesty to her People in Jamaica.

"I am very happy that my sister should be my personal representative at the celebrations to commemorate the independence of your country.

"I remember well my visit some years ago to your lovely island and the warm welcome which you gave to me. My sister who has also visited you before has, I know, greatly looked forward to being with you on this important occasion in Jamaica's history.

"It is with every good wish for the future that I warmly welcome Jamaica to the Commonwealth family of Nations. I am sure that your country, which has already given an example to the world of how people of many varied origins and traditions may live together in harmony, will have a vital contribution to make to the cause of fuller co-operation, understanding, and tolerance far beyond the immediate area of the world in which it is situated.

"I pray that God may bless and keep your country in all the years that lie ahead."

Busta on taxes: *Those who can pay will have to pay more*

That taxation is likely to be increased among people in the higher income brackets, was indicated at the Prime Minister's first Press conference yesterday afternoon at Irvine Hall, University of the West Indies.

In answer to a question from a foreign correspondent about the "haves" and "have-nots" and a reported plan of the Government to tax the rich in order to help the poor, Sir Alexander replied: "Let me be very frank with you: Those who can pay will have to pay a little more taxes".

But when the questioner further inquired how soon the Government intended to put the plan into effect, the Hon. Edward Seaga replied that there would be no answer to this question, as when there were to be tax increases, only two people knew — the Prime Minister and the Minister of Finance.

Ashenheim Ambassador to Washington

Mr. Neville N. Ashenheim, C.B.E., is to be the first Jamaican Ambassador to Washington, it was announced last Saturday from the Premier's Office.

Mr. Ashenheim was a member of the old Legislative Council from 1959 and became Minister without Portfolio and Leader of Government Business following the April 10 general election.

He was not nominated to the newly-constituted Senate which has succeeded the Legislative Council.

Mr. Ashenheim is a solicitor by profession and a director of a number of commercial and industrial companies. He is Chairman of the Board of the Gleaner

MARILYN MONROE FOUND DEAD

Sleeping pills nearby

HOLLYWOOD, August 7 (AP): Blonde and beautiful Marilyn Monroe, a glamorous symbol of the gay, exciting life of Hollywood, died tragically Sunday.

The world may never know whether she deliberately took her life—but a special "suicide team" will have a pretty good idea before it makes a final report on her death.

Her body was found nude in bed, a probable suicide. She was 36.

The long-troubled star clutched a telephone in one hand. An empty bottle of sleeping pills was nearby.

Midnight...then bonfires, fireworks...

Down the Union Jack, up the Black, Gold and Green

With pomp and ceremony, and in an atmosphere of general rejoicing all over the country, Jamaica became an independent nation at midnight Sunday.

More than 20,000 people crowded the National Stadium Sunday night to see the Union Jack hauled down and the Jamaica National Flag hoisted in its place to the top of the flagstaff while eager voices sang the Jamaica National Anthem.

The flag-raising ceremony was duplicated in towns and villages all over Jamaica as well as in Jamaican communities in England and the United States and in various countries in the Western Hemisphere.

Centre of the ceremonies was Her Royal Highness Princess Margaret, representing her sister, the Queen. Apart from gracing all the state ceremonies and less formal occasions with her presence the Princess declared the nation's first Parliament open at Gordon House yesterday morning.

'Out of many...'

Sharing the spotlight of attention was the Hon. Sir Alexander Bustamante, who has become the first Prime Minister of Jamaica, and holds the portfolios of Minister of External Affairs and Minister of Defence as well; and the nation's first Governor General, His Excellency Sir Kenneth Blackburne and Lady Blackburne.

The spectacle of bonfires on the hills, fireworks at the National Stadium and other centres, dancing in the streets, donkey races, treats for schoolchildren and the aged, regattas, parties galore, brought Jamaicans of all races, all classes and colours and creeds together to celebrate their independence and to symbolise the motto: "Out of many, one people."

Scores of distinguished visitors including Vice-President Lyndon Johnson of the United States, the Rt. Hon. Hugh Fraser, Minister of Aviation in

(Please turn to Page 2, col. 1)

Plea for UN membership

Jamaica applied on Monday, Independence Day, for membership of the United Nations. The application was made by the Prime Minister and Minister of External Affairs, Hon. Sir Alexander Bustamante. In his application Sir Alexander said:

"On behalf of the Government of Jamaica and in my capacity as Minister of External Affairs, I have the honour to inform you that Jamaica having today attained independence, wishes herewith to make application for membership of the United Nations with all the rights and duties attached thereto.

"I should accordingly, be grateful if this application could be submitted to the Security Council at its next meeting... Jamaica accepts the obligation contained in the charter of the United Nations and solemnly undertakes to fulfil them."

From Macmillan — Jamaica equal partner with UK

The Hon. Hugh Fraser, Air Minister and former Under-Secretary of State for the Colonies, handed the following message from the Rt. Hon Harold Macmillan, Prime Minister of the United Kingdom, to ... Sir Alexander Bustamante, the Premier of Jamaica on Sunday morning, August 5:

"I have asked Mr. Fraser, who is leading the British Delegation to the Jamaican Independence Celebrations, to deliver to you, Mr. Prime Minister, this message of goodwill from the British Government and people:

"The association between your country and ours is of very long standing. We have been associated for 300 years. Today Jamaica takes her place in the new Commonwealth as an equal partner with Britain and twelve other independent sovereign states.

"On this day, so historic for both of us, I send cordial greetings and most sincere good wishes to you, your Government, and all the people of Jamaica, for the future of your country. We look forward with confidence to the continuation in new fields of the friendship and understanding which have marked for so many years the association of Jamaica and Brit-

LAUGH IT OFF

"Who's the lucky man?"

Prime Minister's message:

I know you will respond to the challenge

Sir Alexander Bustamante Prime Minister of Jamaica, in a special message to the people of Jamaica on the occasion of the island's attainment of Independence, said yesterday, that he spoke with pride and courage.

Sir Alexander's message follows:

I speak to Jamaicans, both at home and overseas, as the Prime Minister of the Govern- ... will respond to the challenge of this new era on which we now enter and to the difficult tasks and heavy responsibilities ahead of us. Independence means the ... should be proud of the example of racial harmony which we have set for the rest of the world. ... Almighty God for this great day, go forward together into the future with faith, courage and dedication. Let us resolve always to help those less fortunate

Raising of the Jamaican flag

The streets of downtown Kingston presented a picture of multi-coloured brilliance when thousands of decorative electric light bulbs were illuminated to usher in the Jamaica Independence Celebrations.

The brilliant illumination of King Street, downtown Kingston is shown by this photograph taken in the early hours of Jamaica's Independence on the night of Sunday, August 5, 1962.

A solemn Pontifical mass which marks the island's Independence was celebrated at the Holy Trinity Cathedral.

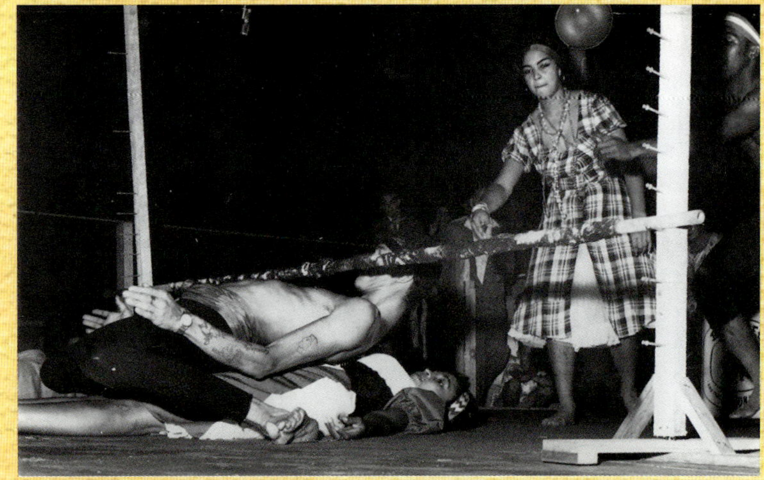

The Limbo Group from Kingston dance at the Independence Jamboree sponsored by Kaiser Bauxite, and held at Pepper, St. Elizabeth on Sunday, August 5, 1962.

A donkey cart plays the part of an escort to the Float Parade put on by the citizens of Hermitage, St. Andrew, as part of their Independence celebrations on August 6, 1962. Here the cart precedes the Float along Violet Avenue in Mona Heights.

FREEDOM JIG: Completely captured by the spirit of Independence, a woman dances by herself during the street dancing held at Grants Pen Road. The music for her "solo" was provided by Count Ossie and his band.

This was the scene at Grants Pen Road with persons celebrating Independence Day on Monday, August 6, 1962, by dancing in the streets. In the background is the truck on which Count Casie and his band provided the music for the happy folk to twist, jive and rock.

A section of the crowd, estimated at 5,000, which attended the St Thomas Parish Fete at Lyssons Recreation Centre, near Morant Bay, on Thursday, August 9, 1962, for the Independence celebration. At right is the Royal Canadian Navy Band, led by Bandmaster Ernest Spiers, rendering one of its pieces.

A happy group at a function held by the East Indian Progressive Society to mark Jamaica's Independence celebrations on August 7, 1962 at Varma Hall.

HER EXCELLENCY LADY CAMPBELL, wife of the Governor-General (second from right), joins a group at cocktails on August 4, 1963, just after the Prime Minister, the Hon. Sir Alexander Bustamante (third from right), had officially declared the JBC-TV service open.

Others from left are Mr Joe Pinchin, member of the JBC board, Lady Bustamante, Mr J. B. Wheeler and Mr A. L. Hendricks, general manager of JBC.

Sir Alex opens television service

Television broadcasting began officially in Jamaica on Sunday evening, just seven months after negotiations were concluded by the Government for the Jamaican Broadcasting Corporation to establish the service.

Witnessing the opening ceremony was a packed JBC studio of dignitaries of Church and State, headed by Their Excellencies the Governor-General, Sir Clifford Campbell, who addressed the gathering, and Lady Campbell.

The service was declared open by the Prime Minister, the Hon. Sir Alexander Bustamante, who expressed the hope that it would go from strength to strength as it discharged its duty for the welfare of the community: of disseminating news, providing wholesome entertainment and through its educational programmes serving the best interest of the nation.

The ceremony was also marked by the receipt of a message from HRH Princess Margaret who, with her husband, sent "best wishes on this the occasion of the inauguration of your television service."

Mr. A. L. Hendriks, general manager of JBC, presided over the proceedings, which were almost wholly televised and during which several congratulatory addresses were delivered.

The advantages

TELEVISING PART OF THE PROGRAMME for the opening of the television service in Jamaica on Sunday evening in a small studio at JBC, Mr. A. L. Hendriks JBC general manager; His Excellency the Governor-General, Sir Clifford Campbell, the Hon. Edward Seaga, Minister of Development and Welfare, Mr. Norman Manley, Leader of the Opposition, (reading from left) await their turn while Mr. James Coltart, chairman of the JBC-TV consortium, speaks before the cameras. Below Mr. Hendriks (left) and Mr. Coltart are seen on the screen.

It's

1963

'Miss Jamaica' Wins Miss World Title

"I never expected to win," she said. "I thought Miss United Kingdom would win."

"Miss World", Jamaica's Carol Joan Crawford is escorted up the red-carpeted aisle of the Ward Theatre by the mayor of the Corporate Area, Councillor Leonard Currey, as she arrives to attend the civic reception in her honour at the Ward Theatre on November 26, 1963. Walking immediately behind is the acting town clerk, Mr. Basil Daniels.

1963

Decorate with [brand] for good

The Daily Gleaner

LARGEST CIRCULATION

Price: FOURPENCE

●Palisadoes Airport ceremony marks inauguration...

AIR JAMAICA FLIES

NATIONAL AIRLINE OPENS SERVICE WITH U.S.

Boeings make inward, outward trips

Heavily booked

SKULL-AT-TANK PROBE

Flour shares offer closing earlier than planned

BOAC's separate U.S.-Jamaica service ends

Kaiser grandson found dead in Rhine

ARMY SPEEDS MAIL-SORTING

Eleven die in UK fires

Newsman attacked at JLP conference

RED PEAS IMPORT HALVES PRICE IN RURAL MARTS

Double-killing in Trinidad

Princess Anne remains in hospital

Three perish in bus crash

Collision kills 6 in car

DID YOU KNOW

THAT FOR LESS THAN

£35

YOU CAN ENJOY

5 full-length movies may be shot here

LAUGH IT OFF

For Extra Long Life, Extra Safety! DUNLOP CYCLE TYRES

SALUTE TO AIR JAMAICA

The Sunday Gleaner

MAY 1, 1966

SALUTE TO AIR JAMAICA

AIR JAMAICA FLIES TODAY

Jamaica's National Airline

Today — Sunday, May 1, 1966 — sees aviation history being written by Jamaica. It witnesses the beginning of operations of a new airline, which starts flying today to take its place among the air fleets of the world.

Air Jamaica, the national airline of this country, has been in the making for four years now — ever since 1962 when Jamaica became an independent nation. Now, after long and careful preparation, it gets off the ground — to open a new chapter in the progress and development of the island.

Jamaica is a partner with British Overseas Airways Corporation and British West Indian Airways in the new airline which is operating between Jamaica and the New York and Miami gateways of the United States of America.

Air Jamaica Inaugural Flight

1966

Saturday, February 1, 1969.
Sunrise 6.40 a.m.
Sunset 6.02 p.m.
Moonrise 5.26 p.m.
Moonset 6.09 a.m.
Full Moon Feb. 2
Last Quarter Feb. 9
New Moon Feb. 16
First Quarter Feb. 23

The Daily Gleaner

LARGEST CIRCULATION — ESTABLISHED 1834 — Price: FIVEPENCE

Tides for Sunday, February 2, 1969.

	High	Low
Pt. Mor.	10.17 a.m.	1.17 a.m.
	6.06 p.m.	3.00 p.m.
Pt. Royal	11.05 a.m.	1.58 a.m.
	7.47 p.m.	2.40 p.m.
MoBay	11.38 a.m.	3.33 a.m.
	8.10 p.m.	4.14 p.m.
St. A's Bay	10.50 a.m.	2.55 a.m.
	7.35 p.m.	3.37 p.m.

Vol. CXXXV. No. 27. — KINGSTON, JAMAICA, SATURDAY, FEBRUARY 1, 1969. — TWENTY-SIX PAGES

STOCK EXCHANGE OPENED

Seaga: Chance for public to make investments

OPPORTUNITY FOR COMPANIES TO RAISE CAPITAL, TOO

TWO OBJECTIVES for the Jamaica Stock Exchange — the opening up of the capital [...]ket for the assistance of companies in Jamaica, and the opening of the doors of those [...]panies to Jamaican investors — were named by the Minister of Finance and Planning, the [...] Edward Seaga, yesterday afternoon.

Declaring open the Exchange, which will start trading on Monday morning, Mr. Seaga said it was the hope of the Government that the Exchange would provide the opportunity for private companies to go public, so as to allow members of the community to have a share in the ownership of the means of production of the country.

Mr. Seaga said it was about four months ago that there was a ceremony to mark the inauguration of the Jamaica Stock Exchange, which took place on September 16 last year. Now, they were marking the formal opening of the Jamaica Stock Exchange and the start of trading activities which would take place on Monday next.

During the interval from September to now, he said, the Jamaica Stock Exchange had formulated the rules under which it would operate, and a great deal of co-operation had taken place between the parties who had a vital interest in the matter

These included the Bank of Jamaica, the Ministry of Finance, and the brokers, who with the "invaluable assistance" of Mr. Mansell Ketchin, of the Toronto Stock Exchange, who was loaned to Jamaica for the purpose, had succeeded in putting together all the rules and regulations which would govern the activities of the Exchange in the coming years.

Background

Giving the background to the establishment of the Exchange, Mr. Seaga said it had not suddenly arisen. The market had been steadily growing. In 1963, the value of new issues on the market totalled £200,000. The value of new issues in 1967, four years later, was £1.5 million, an increase of over seven times.

With regard to the secondary market, the number of new issues in 1963 was 700. The number of new issues in the secondary market in 1967 was 1,800, two and a half times as many. The market had risen in four years from £600,000 to £2½ million.

"A stock exchange cannot exist without a market. This market has been in the process of building up over the past two years and now at last it has arrived," he declared.

Mr. Seaga went on to point out that in 1963 the number of companies that were in a position to offer shares to the public was 16. In 1967, the number had risen to 31 companies. He was pleased to say that nearly all these companies would be listed on the Jamaica Stock Exchange.

"This growth of transactions in stocks is something that is of great value, great promise and great assistance for the development of the country," he declared.

Auction room

Mr. Seaga said a stock exchange was nothing more than an auction room in which certain operations took place under certain rules and regulations. But th[ere] was a second purpose behind the operation of an exchange, and that was to provide an opportunity for those members of the public who sought to make investment, and to those companies which sought to raise capital.

With a stock exchange, private companies which required capital could go on the market to obtain that capital. At the same time, there was provided an opportunity for members of the public, through subscriptions to the capital market, to own a piece of the means of production in the economy of their country.

Mr. Seaga endorsed remarks which had been made earlier by the Governor of the Bank of Jamaica, the Hon. G. Arthur Brown, who is also chairman of the council of the Jamaica Stock Exchange, concerning the "democratization" of businesses in Jamaica.

"As we get more closely to being categorized among the developed countries of the world," Mr. Seaga said, "we have to seek means of spreading the ownership of bu[...] among as many members [...] public as is possible."

One of the means of [...]ing this, he said, was [...] of the Unit Trust, whi[...]mitted the average inve[...] invest his money witho[...]cessarily possessing the [...]ment intelligence to [...] what was a right inv[...] to make; and which h[...] do through a properl[...]ganized institution, suc[...] Unit Trust.

Progress was being ma[de] [in] the establishment of [a] Trust in Jamaica, he [said]. Someone had been found with the necessary ability and experience to operate it, and it was hoped that arrangements would soon be finalized for that person to come to Jamaica and start the Trust.

Here Mr. Seaga stated the two main objectives of the Stock Exchange; and then went on to speak of the need for providing an opportunity for Jamaicans overseas to invest in Jamaica — something that the Stock Exchange could not easily do, but which was a role that could be admirably filled by Jamaican banks opening overseas branches.

Mr. Seaga closed by thanking Mr. Ketchin for coming to Jamaica and giving the Jamaica Stock Exchange the benefit of his "wisdom and experience."

(Continued on Page 8)

STOCK EXCHANGE STARTS: The Minister of Finance and Planning, the Hon. Edward Seaga, at the board of the Jamaica Stock Exchange yesterday afternoon, after he had declared it open and taken part in the first transaction. Looking on (from right) are three stockbroker-members of the Exchange — Messrs. Tony Lloyd, Raglan Golding and Edward Gayle; and, at left, Sir Neville Ashenheim (background), Mr. Karl Richards, Mr. Earle Maynier and Mr. Stanley Motta.

First in island's history . . .

BNS Jamaica setting up branch in UK

A BRANCH of the Bank of Nova Scotia Jamaica Limited is to be established in London, the first branch of a Jamaican-based bank to be set up overseas.

This was announced officially and on behalf of the bank, by the Minister of Finance and Planning, the Hon. Edward Seaga, speaking at the opening of the Jamaica Stock Exchange yesterday afternoon.

Mr. Seaga said the Ministry of Finance and the Bank of Jamaica had been having talks with local banking interests with a view to having such a branch established, in order to encourage Jamaicans overseas to invest in Jamaica.

"I want to congratulate publicly the Bank of Nova Scotia Jamaica Limited for having taken the decision to establish a branch of the bank in the United Kingdom," he said.

Many things had been said, observed, about Jamaicans who lived abroad. But one thing was certain: that those Jamaicans who obtained the opportunity to live and work abroad were well known for their ability to save and for their desire to invest.

More than that, they wished to invest in Jamaica and wanted an opportunity to discuss their investment with Jamaican advisers.

"Only recently in September when I was last in London, members of the Jamaican community there expressed the hope that there would be established in the U.K. and es-

(Continued on Page 8)

Kingston — 50 years ago
•
Russian platform in space
•
Negro America
•
What's your attitude to life?
•
See . . . tomorrow's
SUNDAY GLEANER

SPELLING BEE STARTS TODAY

The tenth annual **Children's Own** Spelling Bee opens today. From now until **February 28**, schools which are qualified subscribers to the **Children's Own** newspaper may choose their champions to represent them at the Parish Finals.

Preparatory, primary and secondary schools in every parish will compete. Nearly 450 schools have gained qualification by being paid-up subscribers to the **Children's Own** newspaper since last term. A list of these schools was published in the January 31 edition of the paper.

The largest number of schools which will compete in a parish is 76, in St. Andrew. Clarendon claims the next largest group of qualified schools with 46. St. Elizabeth follows with 42. In St. Ann there will be 34 and Kingston 33.

Notification

Now that the contest is open, teachers in qualified schools should conduct their competitions to choose the champions according to the rules of the Spelling Bee Handbook. In each school where there are boys and girls, there is one boy champion and one girl champion in a school with boys-only or girls-only, there is just one champion.

Competitors should be under 14 years old at the time when the contest opens, that is, February 1, 1969.

Teachers are advised that as soon as school champions have been chosen, the names and the ages of the winners should be sent **by telegram** to Spelling Bee, Box 40, Kingston.

This year's standard of competition will no doubt be of even keener standard than previous years, as there is the added incentive for parish champions and teachers of a sightseeing trip to Miami.

This tenth anniversary bonus is being given by the Gleaner Company Ltd., publishers of the CHILDREN'S OWN newspaper, and will come at the end of the All-Island Finals in August.

Besides the big prizes of the final week of the Spelling Bee, there are rewards all along for almost every competitor. Each school champion receives a book prize and certificate of merit. Parish champions and runners-up receive additional book prizes.

Perhaps the greatest prize of all is the fun and excitement shared by children and teachers all over the island, now that it is Spelling Bee time again.

'The Last American'

is a 24-part series by Don Oakley, illustrated by John Lane, which will commence in the

GLEANER

on Monday.

•

It will trace the 350-year history of the Negro in North America, with all its ups and downs, light and shade, outstanding and ordinary black people struggling for recognition and equality.

Six believed strangled

RINGKOEBING, Denmark, Jan. 31 (Reuters):

A man, his wife and their five sons aged six to 14, were found dead on their farm near here today.

Police said they believed the farmer strangled his wife and children before shooting himself.

Trade Minister off to Trinidad . . .

Carifta Jamaica's top concern—Lightbourne

THE MINISTER of Trade and Industry, the Hon. Robert Lightbourne, shortly before his departure to the 5th conference of Heads of Commonwealth Caribbean countries in Port-of-Spain by BWIA flight yesterday, said that Jamaica's main concern would be with the Caribbean Free Trade Area.

"My main purpose is not to deal with the Regional Bank; the main concern is to see that CARIFTA is strengthened and no impatience or undue haste causes any damage to it," he said.

Mr. Lightbourne, who will lead Jamaica's delegation to the conference, was being asked what stand Jamaica would be taking at the meeting concerning the Regional Bank.

An issue developed over the Bank after the Hon. Edward Seaga, Minister of Finance and Planning, walked out of a meeting in Antigua last April in protest against Barbados being selected for the site instead of Jamaica.

Since then a number of member territories have been expressing the fear that CARIFTA would fail if the matter was not resolved and the Bank become a reality.

Absence of PM

Mr. Lightbourne is leading Jamaica's delegation to the conference, which will be from February 3 to 6, in the absence of the Prime Minister who is unable to attend.

When Mr. Lightbourne left yesterday he was accompanied by his Personal Assistant, Mr. Peter King, and the Principal Assistant Secretary in his Ministry, Mr. Don Bryce. He has gone ahead of the rest of the delegation in order to have preliminary talks with the Heads of other participating territories before the beginning of the conference.

The other member of the delegation, Dr. Neville Gallimore, Parliamentary Secretary in the Ministry of External Affairs; also Mr. James M. Lloyd, Permanent Secretary, Ministry of External Affairs and the Hon. G. Arthur Brown, Governor of the Bank of Jamaica, who will be advisers, will be leaving tomorrow.

Other advisers to the delegation will be Sir Egerton Richardson, Jamaica's Ambassador to the United States, who is special adviser to the Prime Minister on international affairs and Mr. Ivo DeSouza, Jamaica's High Commissioner to Trinidad and Tobago, (whose alternative will be Mr. Gordon Wells).

Mr. Lightbourne was seen off by officials of his Ministry — Mr. Alva Ross, Parliamentary Secretary; Mr. Herbert Walker, Permanent Secretary and Mr. Pat Mullings, Principal Assistant Secretary.

LAUGH IT OFF

"That's funny. In my family my wife also handles the money."

Hill too busy for trip to Venezuela

The Minister of Public Utilities and Housing, the Hon. Wilton Hill, has announced that owing to pressure of work he has had to forego his visit to Venezuela to take part in the Second Inter-American Housing Congress scheduled to last from today to February 10.

For the same reason he has decided that his two senior officers who were to accompany him, Mr. W. A. McDonald, acting Permanent Secretary and Mr. H. Bent, acting Assistant Under Secretary will also be unable to make the trip.

The Minister has however, decided to send Miss Pauline Maloney, welfare officer who will be in charge of the Sociological Section of the Ministry as he considers that she is likely to derive great benefit from attending the congress.

—JIS

Local Govt. poll date to be set Monday

Gleaner Political Reporter

Passage by the Senate yesterday of the Bills amending the KSAC and Parish Council laws to permit the Government to call Local Government General Elections before June 21, this year, has cleared the way for early elections for these councils.

The Bills go to the Governor General today for his assent and the Cabinet on Monday will decide the dates of the election.

It is expected that announcements will be made by the Government immediately following the Cabinet meeting.

The law requires a period of 28 days between nominations and election day, and since announcements of forthcoming elections are not usually made before, say, one week in advance of Nomination Day, the likelihood at the moment is that the KSAC and Parish Council elections will be called for a date in March.

• What the Senate did •

Gleaner Parliamentary Reporter

The Senate yesterday passed two Bills enabling the Government to hold Municipal and Parochial General Elections before June 21, this year.

The Bills, piloted through the Senate by the Minister of State, the Hon. Hector Wynter, were passed by the House of Representatives on Wednesday, and go to the Governor General today for his assent, and final passage into law.

A third Bill passed by the Senate yesterday, at the instance of the Leader of Government Business, the Hon. Sir Neville Ashenheim, amends the Interpretation Law in respect of the definition of "Minister" to clear the legal way for the transfer of the subject of Work Permits from the Ministry of Home Affairs to the Ministry of Labour and National Insurance, among other things.

The Senate will meet next on Friday next week.

Valentine now member of MCC

It has been officially announced in London that Alfred Valentine, former Jamaica and West Indies cricketer has been appointed a life member of the Marylebone Cricket Club.

This was stated last night by Mr. Neville Smith, assistant secretary of the Jamaica Cricket Board of Control.

The appointment was made for Valentine's "distinguished service to world cricket," Mr. Smith said.

FIFTEEN Iraqis in the dock hearing death sentences passed on Monday by a Revolutionary Court for spying for Israel. Nine of them were Jews. —A.P.

1969

Capture
Sweet Moments
in your
OWN SWEET HOME
Get Home in
30
DAYS*
PLUS
UP TO
100%
MORTGAGE
FINANCING
with low monthly payments.
Get Pre-approved today
VISIT jnbank.com
Conditions apply
JN Bank
We'll help you find a way!
A member of the JN Group

Put Fun an Joke Aside!

Fae Ellington

Who is your favourite Jamaican actor or actress? Your answer could very well depend on your age. Between 1962 and 2022, theatre has provided the perfect script for showing how the Jamaican society evolved from being a part of the colonial project into political Independence and, continuing with our journey of self-discovery. "Theatre has been democratised which has resulted in a range of writing and production designed to appeal to a wider audience, more often recognising aspects of our lives," said former theatre critic, Mervyn Morris. The term, theatre, encompasses performances of all artistic genres. However, for the purpose of this article I will concentrate on the role of plays in Jamaica's national development.

Theatre is team effort, so, I have rallied some members of the 'cast' to share this story with you.

> *Theatre as an industry has played a significant (though seemingly unrecognised) role as exemplar of discipline and collective effort.*
> *Plays start on time!*
> *Theatre practitioners work together.*
> **– Owen 'Blakka' Ellis, actor and educator**

Two important traits, punctuality and teamwork, are highlighted by Blakka. Without these, societies fall apart.

The National Pantomime

The national pantomime was first staged by the Little Theatre Movement (LTM) at The Ward Theatre on Boxing Day 1941 with a performance of *Jack and the Beanstalk,* a centuries-old English fairytale. In 1947, *Cinderella* was staged as the national pantomime. The Honourable Louise Bennett Coverley, 'Miss Lou', recently returned from England wrote in her piece in *The Gleaner*, "The Pantomime was pretty, pretty costumes, pretty light and everybody white." *(The Jamaican Theatre, Highlights of the Performing Arts in the Twentieth Century. Wycliffe Bennett and Hazel Bennett).*

The British fairytale pantomimes eventually gave way to Jamaican stories using our language. Actors, such as Miss Lou, Ranny Williams, Leonie Forbes and Charles Hyatt, also brought colour to the national pantomimes.

The Emerging Jamaican Identity

The search for personhood was not only carried by politicians and academics, but importantly, by the artistic community.

> *Theatre has kept our eyes open and alert, and has offered a lasting portrayal of ourselves and our culture. It provided a critical space for the sharing of messages, asking questions and delivering answers.*
> **– Leonie Forbes, actress**

This 'portrayal' was made possible by the confident, unapologetic use of *di Jamiekan Langwij* by playwrights. And being 'alert' we saw the need for professional training as a complement to talent.

The Jamaica School of Drama was formed under the auspices of the Little Theatre Movement. With time it would become one of the specialisation schools at the Edna Manley College of the Visual and Performing Arts (EMCVPA).

> *From the anticolonial '60s through the dynamic new strategies and challenges of the postcolonial '70s and '80s, social transformations of communities, and contestations of emerging political and economic realities found in the theatre a crucible of popular discourse.*
> **– Eugene Williams, former director of the School of Drama**

Jamaican playwrights, such as Trevor Rhone, Louis Marriott, Easton Lee, Barbara Gloudon, Lloyd Reckord, Basil Dawkins, David Heron, Ginger Knight, Ralph Holness and Dahlia Harris confronted and interrogated critical and sometimes sensitive issues including issues of gender, disabilities and changing values that were not discussed elsewhere.

> *Pantomime (Jamaican theatre) is more than a time to kin teet and pop laugh fe peas soup. It is important to tell our stories and depict characters that reflect ourselves. Being able to laugh at our mistakes and cheer on our successes is how we made it through the past 60 years.*
> **– Anya Gloudon, production co-ordinator at Little Theatre Movement of Jamaica**

Employment

In addition to providing entertainment and an ability to see our many selves, Jamaican theatre has provided employment, seasonal though it might be. Set design and construction, costume design, wardrobe, technicians for lighting, sound, front of house (ticket sales, ushers), backstage (stage managers, stagehands, operators of snack counters) have been among the beneficiaries. Plays keep families afloat and together, create a necessary valve both for patron and player. Theatre contributes to the Gross Domestic Product (GDP).

> *The playwrights and producers who have been active during the past six decades have often presented work which is emblematic of the particular era, hence capturing the mood and essence of that time. Additionally, the exportation and exposure of many of our plays to overseas audiences have also served as an excellent marketing tool for brand Jamaica, giving those audiences yet another reason to catch a flight and make it Jamaica ... again and again.*
>
> **– David Heron, playwright, producer, actor**

It's not uncommon for several local plays to do performances in the US, Canada, UK and throughout the Caribbean.

> *The Jamaican audience both locally and overseas are solid theatre devotees and theatre practitioners are lauded as great cultural ambassadors.*
>
> **– Ruth HoShing, actress**

> *Telling our own stories in our own voices in more sure-footed ways has been a confidence booster for our younger generation assuring them that our nation has the will for self-reliance and self-determination.*
>
> **– Basil L Dawkins, playwright, producer**

In the 60 years of Independence, theatre has played a vital role that could not be done by any other sector. It has clearly represented the best of Jamaica on so many levels. Theatre is an industry, a business and a marketing tool for brand Jamaica. But it needs help from the state – theatre venues, and from corporate Jamaica – sponsorship. As theatre producer and director, the late Wycliffe Bennett said, "If we don't build more theatre venues, we will need to build more prisons."

Fae Ellington, CD, OD is a specialist broadcaster for national events and was a news anchor and programme presenter/producer in radio and television for over 30 years.

Resilience is in our DNA

Christopher Zacca

Jamaica Love ... I wanna feel Jamaica love
Da one yah represent the citizens of Jamaica

The lively sound of Busy Signal's tribute to Jamaica has been playing in my head as I think of the best things about Jamaica. How does such a small country give so much to the world: one of the greatest genres of music, the fastest men and women in track and field, innovators in art, science, and technology, and so much more?

I say it is the resilience of our people.

Jamaica has undergone some serious trials and, yet, somehow, we have managed to survive, and we continue to strive. Our resilience has been displayed consistently through natural disasters from the great Kingston Earthquake at the turn of the last century, to Hurricane Gilbert in 1988. The latter saw Jamaica developing a national disaster preparedness office and becoming a leader in natural disaster management in the Caribbean. The COVID-19 pandemic has shown me that the unswerving resilience of our people is what makes this 'little place' called Jamaica 'larger than life'.

Resilience is one's ability to bounce back, that ability to adapt to changes around you, that ability to remain strong in times of stress or loss.

I think of my team at Sagicor Group Jamaica, who, despite the challenges of working online for an extended period, managed to transfer the energy of face-to-face engagement to online with such ease, and executed our 50th anniversary virtually with excellence and zeal, delivering a world-class series of events. That is resilience. The Sagicor team is a kind of microcosm of the Jamaican people, accepting what is and doing all they can to make it better for themselves and their families.

I see resilience in the innovation of the handcart man who created a vehicle for transporting goods in the market with ease. I see it in the young men and women who train every day to represent their schools at Champs while balancing the demands of their schoolwork. I see it in the doctors at the Kingston Public Hospital who beat the odds of limited equipment and continue to save the lives of patients daily. I saw resilience in the 1988 bobsleigh team who left a tropical place for Winter Olympics in Calgary, Canada and the subsequent teams who continue to represent their country in weather conditions they are unaccustomed to. It is this resilience that made Novelene Williams Mills win a bronze after learning she had breast cancer at the 2012 Olympics.

The resilience of the Jamaican people is the spirit of Marcus Garvey; it is the spirit of Nanny of the Maroons and Sam Sharpe, who fought for their freedom with all their might. It is in Bob Marley and all the artists and players of music who even "when the going gets tough and the tough gets going" do not stop.

I believe there are some common traits in resilient people including our beliefs, our emotional flexibility, and our moral compass. Resilient people do not dwell on the negative; they look for the opportunities even in their

darkest hour. Even amid the pandemic, Jamaicans were busy making the most out of quarantine. There were beautiful stories of ones with very little for themselves giving what they could to make others comfortable. Shop fronts became classrooms, walls became makeshift chalkboards and teachers were sending lessons via WhatsApp to parents' phones for children who did not own a tablet.

Resilience is also the ability to see beyond the now and to have hope that the future is brighter. Psychologists have suggested that there are some common qualities that are evident in resilient people – competence, confidence, connection, character, contribution, coping and control.

I see all of those in the people of Jamaica. We can do anything we decide to and develop the competence through education, wit, or drive. We are a confident people; Usain Bolt beating his chest as he bolts through the finish line is a perfect example of our confidence. Jamaicans thrive on connectedness with one another. From rural districts, to street parties or church, we find ourselves a part of a community. Examples of men and women of exemplary character abound, and we take pride in honesty and integrity of character. The culture of volunteerism is a big part of Jamaica's businesses, schools, churches, and clubs, and is perhaps the best way I can explain our desire to contribute to society. We know how to cope in the most trying circumstances, and best as we can maintain control over our lives.

As we celebrate 60 years of Independence, I dare say it is our resilient spirit that is the very best of Jamaica.

Christopher Zacca is president and CEO at Sagicor Group Jamaica Limited

Best of Jamaica – 60 Years On

Dennis Chung

As Jamaica celebrates 60 years of Independence it is useful to recognise what has helped to put us on the map as a global brand. Certainly, on a per capita basis, we have made a huge global impact. We have the fastest women and men in the world; arguably the best music, and one of the best tourism products in the world. As a result, everyone on this planet knows about this little island of under three million people.

There are so many achievements that can be seen as the 'best of the best' that have made us such a great nation. Naturally many will think of the sporting exploits, music, and tourism, as these are things that readily come to mind when one thinks Jamaica, but, for me, the foundation of Jamaica's greatness is built on our democracy, and more specifically the press freedom we enjoy, as well as the strength of our institutions. We tend to take these for granted especially when we hear and see news of coups, challenges to election results and the murder of journalists in other countries. Yet, these are the pillars that have formed the foundation of Jamaican society and have cemented our place as a global force. We take them for granted, as they seem to have always been around, however, if we think about what happens in other countries we will realise how lucky we are to have these two essential pillars as part of our democracy.

Despite the negatives we are known for, such as the high murder rate, we have been able to produce great men and women in a variety of fields, many from humble backgrounds. Their achievements were possible as a result of access to opportunities made possible by our democratic institutions. It is also arguable that our press freedom and institutions are the reason we might have avoided the economic and social disaster that have befallen many other countries. The proliferation of media houses, which allow citizens to criticise our leadership, and the independence of institutions, such as the Bank of Jamaica, Auditor General's Department, Integrity Commission, Electoral Office of Jamaica, and the public defender, are of note.

To understand this link between environment (press freedom and strong institutions) and greatness, one only has to think of two children growing up in two different environments. The first child is told what he must become when he grows up, whom to marry, what to wear, and is given limited information, such as happens in some countries with censorship. The second child is allowed to learn from all sources, have friends he chooses, is encouraged to pursue his passion, and to openly challenge any ideas he does not agree with. I am sure everyone will agree that the second child has a better chance at greatness.

This is the impact of press freedom and strong institutions on a country.

With this freedom (democracy), of course, there is always the risk that persons (children) left on their own, without proper guidance, will become wayward, which leads to negative consequences for themselves and ultimately the country.

Many will argue that this is what happened to Jamaica, which is a logical argument. Because too many have been left to 'express themselves' coupled with the fact that many politicians are swayed by public opinion, we have developed a society that is lax in regards proper law and order. This has resulted in a high murder rate that has contributed to Jamaica achieving way below its potential. It has also created a situation where our politics has been one of pandering to the crowd rather than doing what is right for our country.

This, however, does not depreciate the value of press freedom and strong institutions that we have created. What it means is that there needs to be a push for better governance, which can be seen as stronger institutions, as it is not a matter of trading one for the other.

This is why for me the best of the best in Jamaica, after 60 years of Independence, are press freedom and our institutions.

Dennis Chung is chairman of the National Solid Waste Management Authority and general secretary of the Jamaica Football Federation

SHARING 60 YEARS OF TOGETHERNESS
Our connections empower the full expression of the love we have for our wonderful culture together. Out of many, there is only ONE JAMAICA.
Nuff love from Flow. Jamaica's Network.
JAMAICA 60
Re-igniting a Nation for Greatness
FLOW

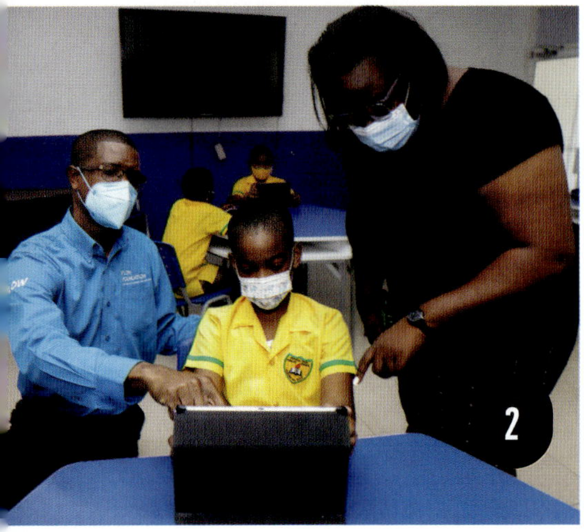

1. *Meeting our customers in their towns and communities*
2. *Powering and supporting digital transformation at Duhaney Park Primary School*
3. *Technician on the job*
4. *Team Flow sending all their love to Jamaica*

FLOW... A PROUD AND STEADFAST PARTNER IN JAMAICA'S DEVELOPMENT

As Jamaica's longest-serving full-service communications and entertainment provider, Flow has been a proud and steadfast partner in our country's development for more than 150 years. During that time, we have remained at the forefront of keeping Jamaicans connected to the world and to one another.

Powering Jamaica & Creating Moments That Matter

The provider of choice for key industries and sectors, we are providing innovative information communication technology (ICT) solutions and delivering superior value while being mindful of the crucial role we play every day.

From traffic lights to point of sale systems, from security systems to empowering businesses, from remote work to online learning, we are playing a pivotal role in driving the digital transformation of our country, including the thousands of small businesses which are the lifeblood of our economy. We are also the proud technological partner behind major critical national imperatives, such as the transformation of our country's health-care system.

Flow has been here every step of the way – also bringing consumers the lowest mobile rates in our history, being the first to bring 3G technology to the market, the first to introduce sophisticated Cable TV services and the first to deliver 90 per cent LTE population coverage.

We are Jamaica's partner for today and the future.

Empowering Our Communities

As we continue to expand the largest fibre network in the country, Flow is focused on enabling the progress of all Jamaicans through digital inclusion as we prepare our fellow citizens for full participation in this digital economy.

Our Flow Foundation has, through hundreds of projects over the decades, helped to bridge the digital divide, supported youth and community development, as well as promoted environmental responsibility across our country while we connected communities and transformed lives.

Now, under our Foundation's flagship programmes, we continue to positively impact lives and institutions.

Through our Skills for the Future programme, thousands are receiving free training and certification in digital and data literacy and similarly, thousands of Jamaicans are also reskilling and upskilling themselves to be more employable or to pursue their own entrepreneurial ventures through our free, certified Training for Professionals Programme.

While we continue to empower one another, we are also providing free fixed broadband service to over 250 schools across the country under our Internet in Schools programme, as well as providing or upgrading broadband service to select community centres, places of safety and health-care facilities.

Our Purpose

As we reflect on the history that has made us a cornerstone of the experiences and achievements which have brought us to where we are today as a country, we are reminded of one of our company's philosophies – 'Our work has purpose and what we do makes a difference'.

This is evident in the work that we do at Flow, connecting thousands of Jamaicans in hundreds of communities, through Jamaica's largest fibre network, to the digital world; the work that we do at our Flow Foundation, educating our fellow Jamaicans and empowering them, so they can navigate the World Wide Web and take advantage of the many opportunities, such as online jobs and career growth opportunities and benefits; and in leveraging our technological backbone and innovative solutions for national development and economic growth.

Looking to The Future

Flow continues to enable and drive progress at the individual, community and national levels, and is inextricably woven into the fabric of Jamaica's history and growth.

As we look to the years ahead, we pledge to continue leading technological advancements across our country, transforming businesses and communities to create more moments that matter and even more possibilities for a brighter future.

Today, our services are underpinned by over 50,000 kilometres of the most modern subsea and terrestrial fibre networks in this part of the world. With a focus on combining the convenience and innovation of mobile with the strength of fixed technology, Flow offers unparalleled connectivity – the fastest broadband with the latest video content, plus best-in-class mobile products allowing our customers to access what matters most to them.

We remain committed to continue to meaningfully impact lives as Jamaica's partner on its journey to a better, more enabled society for its citizens.

5

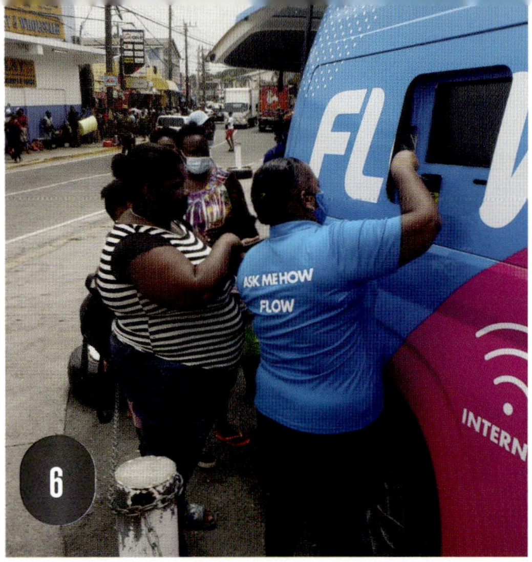

6

7

5. The National Council for Senior Citizens presents the Flow Foundation with its Corporate Service Award in recognition of the organization's work in creating and enabling a supportive environment for seniors

6. Meeting our customers in their towns and communities

7. Team Flow sending all their love to Jamaica

8. Flow Business supporting small businesses with high-speed internet and smart solutions

9. Signing of Contract with the Ministry of Health and Wellness to provide Managed Network Services to support the transformation of health-care in Jamaica

10. C&W Business is presented with a Pioneer Award from the Business Processing Industry Association of Jamaica (BPIAJ) in recognition of its lasting contributions, leadership, enthusiasm, and tireless efforts in supporting the growth and success of the BPO industry

11. Members of the Treasure Beach Women's Group give the thumbs-up as they get ready to embark upon their training under the Skills for the Future Programme

8

9

10

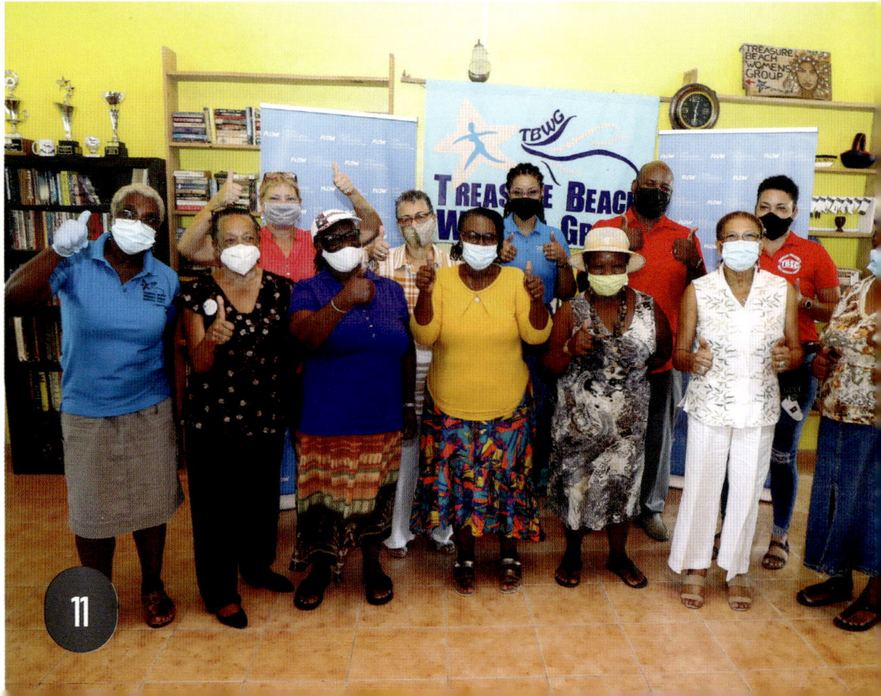

11

JAMAICA MAKES QUALITY GOODS

JAMAICANS are steadily coming into an appreciation of their own, and nowhere is there greater evidence of this than in the field of manufactur which are gaining more and more national acceptance as time passes.

PIONEER INDUSTRY: "Red Stripe" beer being produced in the modern | brewery of Desnoes & Geddes Ltd. in Kingston. | — JIDC The 52-year-old company recently "went public".

As a matter of national pride, as well as of economic practicability, more Jamaicans are "buying Jamaican" — purchasing and patronising the products of Jamaican industry which are coming on to the market with increasing quantity and variety.

An import restriction and substitution policy adopted and enforced by the Government has naturally helped to bring about a change in the former attitude of prejudice on the part of some Jamaicans towards locally-made goods — by giving them, in many cases, no choice of an alternative foreign article.

But the approach of most Jamaicans to their own home-made products has also undergone a significant change because of their growing appreciation of the fact that the products themselves have improved, and that what they are being offered now are, in the great majority of cases, quality products.

So good are many of these products, in fact, that they are able to stand competition and to be sold abroad — as positive a proof of their quality as any other test. Jamaican rum, coffee and cigars have long established themselves throughout the world as top-class products. More recently, products such as beer and liqueurs have helped to enhance Jamaicas' name on the international market.

Coming near home, the manufacturers and exporters. A wide range of Jamaican products are being shipped to the Commonwealth Caribbean territories and finding a good market and ready acceptance among the consumers in those countries.

So it is no question of chauvinism. When Jamaicans buy products made in the island they are assured, 99 percent of the time, that what they are buying is good stuff: that they are not paying any special price for patriotism, but that what they are getting is value for their money.

●

SINCE THE GOVERNMENT of Jamaica decided on industrialization of the country as a national objective, a great deal of development has taken place in this area. As a pioneering body, the Jamaica Industrial Development Corporation has played a great part in bringing manufacturing industry to the island and in developing industrial skills among Jamaicans.

More recently, the Jamaica Manufacturers Association has acted in a dual role, not only in giving positive help and assistance to manufacturers in their local operations, but in assisting them to develop in the export field.

By the highly-successful industrial exhibitions which it has organized from time to time, the J.M.A. has helped to focus national attention on the products made in Jamaica by local manufacturers and to encourage Jamaicans to appreciate and to be proud of the goods turned out by the local factories and plants.

By organized promotional efforts such as the "Flying Showcase" which went to the Eastern Caribbean some years ago, and by the efforts of individual members of the association who make personal promotional trips to the area, the J.M.A. has also played a key role in helping to make Jamaican manufacturers more export-minded and so to develop the market for their products.

More recently, the Jamaican Exporters Association has come along to widen the effort being made to broaden the scope of Jamaican manufacturing industry by breaking into overseas markets. And the Government itself has given recognition to this vital aspect of the "buy Jamaican" attitude by establishing the National Export Council which has the official responsibility to encourage and promote export sales of Jamaican goods.

With the development of the CARIFTA market, more and more Jamaican manufacturers are getting into the export trade. At the same time, Jamaican goods are meeting competition at home from other CARIFTA-made products, which is to the benefit of Jamaican consumers in terms of both quality and price.

MEANWHILE, Jamaican industrial and

(Contd. on Page IV)

PIONEER INDUSTRY: "Red Stripe" beer being produced in the modern brewery of Desnoes & Geddes Ltd. in Kingston. The 52-year-old company recently "went public". — JIDC

— JIDC

MILK PLANT: Production line in the plant of Cremo Ltd., in Kingston, producers of milk and other processed food products.

— JIDC

SALT PLANT: The Minister of Trade and Industry, the Hon. Robert Lightbourne, pressing button to start packaging of refined salt at new $600,000 plant of Alkali Limited near Spanish Town. The International Salt Company of Pennsylvania has an interest in the new company and designed the new plant which utilises the latest equipment.

11 — SATURDAY, MARCH 21, 1970. *THE DAILY GLEANER BUY JAMAICAN SUPPLEMENT*

Foreman vs Frasier Boxing Showdown

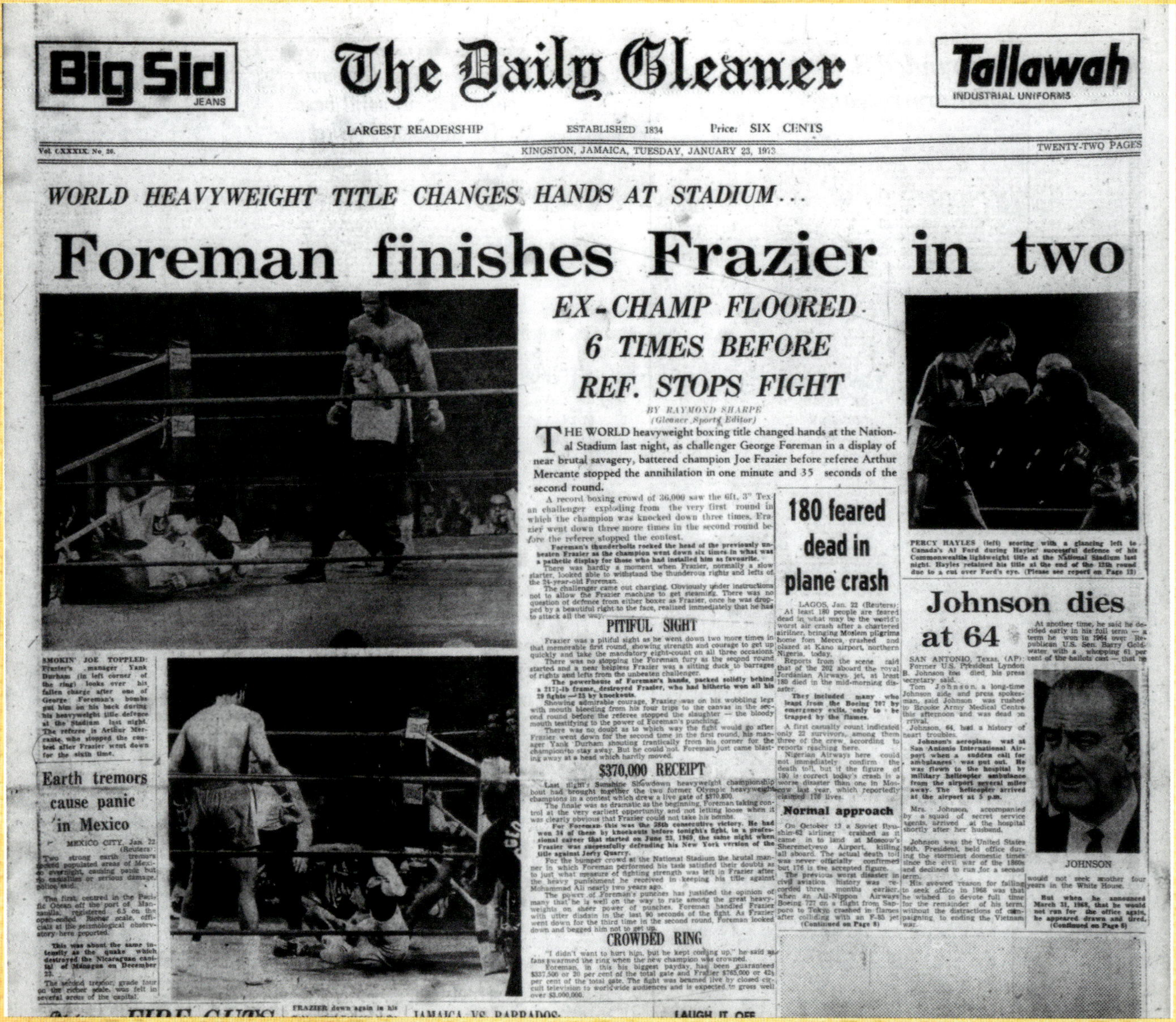

Big Sid JEANS

The Daily Gleaner

Tallawah INDUSTRIAL UNIFORMS

LARGEST READERSHIP ESTABLISHED 1834 Price: SIX CENTS

Vol. CXXXIX. No. 20. KINGSTON, JAMAICA, TUESDAY, JANUARY 23, 1973 TWENTY-TWO PAGES

WORLD HEAVYWEIGHT TITLE CHANGES HANDS AT STADIUM...

Foreman finishes Frazier in two

EX-CHAMP FLOORED 6 TIMES BEFORE REF. STOPS FIGHT

BY RAYMOND SHARPE (Gleaner Sports Editor)

THE WORLD heavyweight boxing title changed hands at the National Stadium last night, as challenger George Foreman in a display of near brutal savagery, battered champion Joe Frazier before referee Arthur Mercante stopped the annihilation in one minute and 35 seconds of the second round.

A record boxing crowd of 36,000 saw the 6ft. 3" Texan challenger exploding from the very first round in which the champion was knocked down three times. Frazier went down three more times in the second round before the referee stopped the contest.

Foreman's thunderbolts rocked the head of the previously unbeaten Frazier as the champion went down six times in what was a pathetic display for those who had installed him as favourite.

There was hardly a moment when Frazier, normally a slow starter, looked able to withstand the thunderous rights and lefts of the 24-year-old Foreman.

The challenger came out charging. Obviously under instructions not to allow the Frazier machine to get steaming. There was no question of defence from either boxer as Frazier, once he was dropped by a beautiful right to the face, realized immediately that he has to attack all the way.

PITIFUL SIGHT

Frazier was a pitiful sight as he went down two more times in that memorable first round, showing strength and courage to get up quickly and take the mandatory eight-count on all three occasions.

There was no stopping the Foreman fury as the second round started and a near helpless Frazier was a sitting duck to barrages of rights and lefts from the unbeaten challenger.

The powerhouse of Foreman's hands, packed solidly behind a 217½-lb frame, destroyed Frazier, who had hitherto won all his 29 fights — 25 by knockouts.

Showing admirable courage, Frazier was on his wobbling legs with mouth bleeding from his four trips to the canvas in the second round before the referee stopped the slaughter — the bloody mouth testifying to the power of Foreman's punching.

There was no doubt as to which way the fight would go after Frazier went down for the second time in the first round, his manager Yank Durham shouting frantically from his corner for the champion to stay away. But he could not. Foreman just came blasting away at a head which hardly moved.

$370,000 RECEIPT

Last night's Sunshine Showdown heavyweight championship bout had brought together the two former Olympic heavyweight champions in a contest which drew a live gate of $370,800.

The finale was as dramatic as the beginning, Foreman taking control at the very earliest opportunity and not letting loose when it was clearly obvious that Frazier could not take his bombs.

For Foreman this was the 38th consecutive victory. He had won 34 of these by knockouts before tonight's fight, in a professional career that started on June 23, 1969, the same night when Frazier was successfully defending his New York version of the title against Jerry Quarry.

For the bumper crowd at the National Stadium the brutal manner in which Foreman performed his task satisfied their doubts as to just what measure of fighting strength was left in Frazier after the heavy punishment he received in keeping his title against Mohammad Ali nearly two years ago.

The power of Foreman's punches has justified the opinion of many that he is well on the way to rate among the great heavyweights on sheer power of punches. Foreman handled Frazier with utter disdain in the last 90 seconds of the fight. As Frazier went down for the third time in the second round, Foreman looked down and begged him not to get up.

CROWDED RING

"I didn't want to hurt him, but he kept coming up," he said as fans swarmed the ring when the new champion was crowned.

Foreman, in this his biggest payday, had been guaranteed $337,500 or 20 per cent of the total gate and Frazier $765,000 or 42½ per cent of the total gate. The fight was beamed live by closed circuit television to worldwide audiences and is expected to gross well over $3,000,000.

SMOKIN' JOE TOPPLED: Frazier's manager Yank Durham (in left corner of the ring) looks over his fallen charge after one of George Foreman's bombs put him on his back during his heavyweight title defence at the Stadium last night. The referee is Arthur Mercante who stopped the contest after Frazier went down for the sixth time.

180 feared dead in plane crash

LAGOS, Jan. 22 (Reuters): At least 180 people are feared dead in what may be the world's worst air crash after a chartered airliner, bringing Moslem pilgrims home fom Mecca, crashed and blazed at Kano airport, northern Nigeria, today.

Reports from the scene said that of the 202 aboard the royal Jordanian Airways jet, at least 180 died in the mid-morning disaster.

They included many who leapt from the Boeing 707 by emergency exits, only to be trapped by the flames.

A first casualty count indicated only 22 survivors, among them three of the crew, according to reports reaching here.

Nigerian Airways here could not immediately confirm the death toll, but if the figure of 180 is correct today's crash is a worse disaster than one in Moscow last year, which reportedly claimed 176 lives.

Normal approach

On October 13 a Soviet Ilyushin-62 airliner crashed as it came in to land at Moscow's Sheremetyevo Airport, killing all aboard. The actual death toll was never officially confirmed but 176 is the accepted figure.

The previous worst disaster in civil aviation history was recorded three months earlier, when an All-Nippon Airways Boeing 727 on a flight from Sapporo to Tokyo crashed in flames after colliding with an F-86 jet

(Continued on Page 8)

PERCY HAYLES (left) scoring with a glancing left to Canada's Al Ford during Hayles' successful defence of his Commonwealth lightweight title at the National Stadium last night. Hayles retained his title at the end of the 12th round due to a cut over Ford's eye. (Please see report on Page 13)

Johnson dies at 64

SAN ANTONIO, Texas, (AP): Former U.S. President Lyndon B. Johnson has died, his press secretary said.

Tom Johnson, a long-time Johnson aide and press spokesman, said Johnson was rushed to Brooke Army Medical Centre this afternoon and was dead on arrival.

Johnson, 64, had a history of heart troubles.

Johnson's aeroplane was at San Antonio International Airport when a sudden call for ambulances was put out. He was flown to the hospital by military helicopter ambulance from the airport several miles away. The helicopter arrived at the airport at 3 p.m.

Mrs. Johnson, accompanied by a squad of secret service agents, arrived at the hospital shortly after her husband.

Johnson was the United States 36th. President, held office during the stormiest domestic times since the civil war of the 1860s and declined to run for a second term.

His avowed reason for failing to seek office in 1968 was that he wished to devote full time for the remainder of his term, without the distractions of campaigning, to ending the Vietnam war.

At another time, he said he decided early in his full term — a term he won in 1964 over Republican U.S. Sen. Barry Goldwater with a whopping 61 per cent of the ballots cast — that he would not seek another four years in the White House.

JOHNSON

But when he announced March 31, 1968, that he would not run for the office again, he appeared drawn and tired.

(Continued on Page 6)

Earth tremors cause panic in Mexico

MEXICO CITY, Jan. 22 (Reuters): Two strong earth tremors rocked populated areas of Mexico overnight, causing panic but no casualties or serious damage, police said.

The first, centred in the Pacific Ocean off the port of Manzanillo, registered 6.5 on the open-ended Richter scale, officials at the seismological observatory here reported.

This was about the same intensity as the quake which destroyed the Nicaraguan capital of Managua on December 23.

The second tremor, grade four on the richter scale, was felt in several areas of the capital.

1973

The Daily Gleaner

LARGEST READERSHIP ESTABLISHED 1834 Price: FIFTEEN CENTS

Vol. CXLI No. 256. KINGSTON, JAMAICA, THURSDAY, OCTOBER 30, 1975 FORTY PAGES

MINIMUM WAGE ORDER APPROVED BY HOUSE

NEW LAW COMES INTO EFFECT ON SUNDAY

GLEANER PARLIAMENTARY REPORTER

THE HOUSE OF Representatives voted approval of the National Minimum Wage Order yesterday after an abortive Opposition attempt to move for a two-tiered minimum of $20 for household helps and $26.50 for other workers.

Minister of Labour and Employment the Hon. Ernest Peart formally moved for approval of the order which goes into effect November 2, setting a national minimum of $20 for a 40-hour work week.

Certain objections to the Order were stated for the Opposition by the Rt. Hon. Hugh Shearer protesting the exclusion of rural bus workers and task workers from the ambit of the Order and the level of a single minimum wage coupling household helps with others in industry and commerce.

IN-DEPTH STUDY

At the conclusion of the debate the Minister gave an assurance that the Minimum Wage Advisory Commission was undertaking an in-depth study of the rural transport situation to make recommendations on minimum rates for all categories of workers in the industry.

Mr. Peart said that the Rural Bus and Stage Carriage Association had given him an assurance that they will award some increase in wage rates from November 2 – the day the Order comes into effect.

The Minister also said that at a later stage a separate order would be considered for task workers and consideration would also be given to giving premium pay to hourly paid workers for Sunday work as suggested by Mr. Shearer.

Mr. Shearer had sought to embody the Opposition's objections in the form of an amendment of the Order but the Speaker ruled that such an amendment could not be entertained.

Mr. Speaker said that having regard to the fact that the principal law was amended in November 1974, requiring the

(Cont'd on Page 20)

In the House:

Robotham named to committee

Gleaner Parliamentary Reporter

An additional government member was named yesterday to the constitutional review committee to make it five Government to three Opposition members.

The Hon. Keble Munn presented the relevant motion naming Dr. Upton Robotham, Parliamentary Secretary in the Ministry of Education, to the committee.

The House approved the motion after some argument by the Hon. Robert Lightbourne about the basis for establishing that ratio of membership.

The committee is due to meet this morning to deal with a bill seeking a constitutional amendment to increase the number of Senators who may be made ministers and also assigned portfolios.

In other business the House approved the National Minimum Wage Order, 1975.

The Minister of Health made a statement on the death of a baby in the Mandeville Hospital last week.

The adjournment was taken at 5:35 p.m. until 2 p.m. today.

Granted appeal leave

LONDON, Oct. 29 (Reuters): Donald Parkes who has been sentenced to death for murder by a Jamaican court, was granted special leave to appeal against conviction by the Privy Council Judicial Committee today.

But the committee dismissed a petition by Vincent McFarquhar, seeking leave to appeal against a murder conviction for which he has been sentenced to death.

Parkes was sentenced to death by Jamaica's Home Circuit Court in January last year after being convicted of the murder in 1971 of 32 year-old Daphne Graham, of Beynes Road, ST. Andrew. The Privy Council was told that the case for the Prosecution rested on circumstantial evidence.

Wrong direction

Counsel for Parkes said that the trial judge, the Chief Justice, had given a wrong direction to the Jury. This was that Parkes' silence when accused of stabbing Miss Graham, was a matter which could be taken account in deciding whether Parkes had in fact stabbed her.

Gerald Davies, contesting the appeal petition on behalf of the Crown, submitted that once evidence was admissible it was open to the Judge to make any comment he liked upon it.

An application by Parkes for leave to appeal against the conviction was dismissed by the Jamaica court of Appeal in July 1974.

READY FOR MAY PEN-KINGSTON RUN: This is one of the rail cars which has been readied for the May Pen to Kingston route, being introduced by the Jamaica Railway Corporation on a three-month trial basis, beginning on Saturday. It is powered by a Rolls Royce diesel engine with 315 Horse Pywer and can carry 88 passengers.

SUMMONS SERVED ON DUNCAN

The general secretary of the People's National Party, Dr. D. K. Duncan, was yesterday served with a summons by the police in connection with a recent incident in which woman constable Maxine Malcolm received injuries.

Charging Dr. Duncan with assault occasioning bodily harm to Woman Constable Maxine Malcolm, the summons is returnable in the St. Mary Resident Magistrate's Court on November 6. It was served on Dr. Duncan in Kingston.

The development has followed a ruling by the Director of Public Prosecutions to whose office statements in the incident were submitted.

The Clerk of the Courts St. Mary had taken the decision that she would prefer that the matter of prosecution be dealt with by the D.P.P.

Miss Malcolm was in hospital in Port Maria for several days after an alleged assault at the courthouse building during the recent St. Mary by-election.

She was discharged but readmitted to the hospital on Sunday, and is still a patient there.

STATEMENT BY THE GLEANER CO. LTD.

The Production workers of the Gleaner Company Ltd. went on a three hour "protest demonstration" yesterday from 9.15 a.m. to 12.15 p.m. Fifteen minutes after resumption they punched out for lunch, reporting back for work at 1.30 p.m.

The Management of the company met at the Ministry of Labour and Employment on Tuesday afternoon with Mr. L. Beckford of the B.I.T.U. and certain worker delegates, to discuss rates of pay for certain categories of workers who are being retrained in the new production process.

The meeting ended at the Ministry with the understanding that the parties would meet again on Wednesday, 5th November, to continue the discussion. The B.I.T.U. has not indicated to the company the reasons for the protest demonstration by the workers.

The STAR which normally is published between 1.00 and 1.30 p.m. was not ready for printing up to 4.30 p.m. yesterday, so publication had to be abandoned. The company expresses regret to the public for any inconvenience suffered.

Found dead with gun in hand

The body of Mr. Frederick Mills, 75-year-old landed proprietor and retired J.P., was found yesterday morning at the lawn of his home at Kempshot in St. James. The police belive that he committed suicide.

Hurrying from the house at the sound of an explosion, members of his family made the find. A bullet wound was to the head and his revolver was clutched in his hand.

LICENCE FOR CARICOM GOODS CAUSING CONFUSION — *JMA*

THE JAMAICA Manufacturers Association has said that as a result of Mr. Patterson's announcement in Guyana of licencing requirements for Caricom imports, the Caricom spirit is now degenerating "to total hostility hostility", amidst current confusion and threatened dislocation.

JMA President, Mr. Douglas Vaz, in a statement yesterday on behalf of the Association re-stated the association's commitment to the concept of Caricom outlined in the written agreement and called for a tangible demonstration of the "spirit intended therein" by its signatories.

The JMA statement said:

"Following the announcement in Guyana by industry Minister, P.J. Patterson of the imposition of licence requirements for Caricom imports into Jamaica, much confusion has prevailed and some dislocation is threatened.

"The JMA strongly deprecates this external announcement of a Jamaican policy when no prior discussion was held by the Minister locally with the productive sector. Even more to be deprecated is the fact that the productive sector was in almost continuous dialogue (?) with the Government concerning economic stabilisation methods for the preceeding two months. Double standards of this type only double the rate of the erosion of confidence and credibility, which some are trying so hard to rebuild.

"Much concern has been evoked within Caricom as a result of this decision by the Jamaican Government. The JMA has been forewarned that this concern is to be vociferously conveyed to the annual general meeting of the Caribbean Association of Industry and Commerce, now being held in Grenada and at which the JMA is represented by its secretary, Eddie Hall.

"While the JMA is in agreement with the need for licences as a foreign exchange monitoring tool and in fact advocated the use of licences, for this purpose, the tying of

(Cont'd on Page 20)

LAUGH IT OFF

"I'm supposed to see my dentist twice a year."

Ramphal at CPA meeting . . .

PRIORITY URGED FOR S. AFRICAN PROBLEM

NEW DELHI, Oct. 29, (REUTERS): THE COMMONWEALTH must give top priority to the problem of white minority regimes in Southern Africa, Commonwealth Secretary General Sridath Ramphal said here today.

Addressing 300 delegates from 34 nations attending a Commonwealth parliamentary conference, Ramphal said the Commonwealth had to stir the conscience of mankind "for as long as human dignity remained affronted in Southern Africa."

National liberation movements in Africa now were less united and this was regrettable because unity was of critical importance, he said." This will not make the search for solutions any easier," he added.

Several delegates in a debate on Africa expressed support for armed struggle against white regimes there.

Arap Keino of Kenya said; "we fully support the armed struggle for the total freedom of African people." He accused South African and Rhodesian leaders of not being serious about negotiations.

Deserves support

British Labour Party delegate James Johnson said violent struggles were inevitable if peaceful negotiations failed, though a blood bath was too terrible to contemplate.

"The African majority deserves all support, in every form in their movement. We should support them and back them to the hilt," he said.

Guyana's Minister for Parliamentary Affairs, B. Ramsaroop, called on Britain to use military intervention to end the white regime in Rhodesia and rejected Johnson's statement that the time was not opportune for unilateral action by Britain.

Ramphal in his speech also appealed to nations to eradicate world poverty with a new world economic order. Nearly 1,000 million of the world's poorest people subsisted on incomes of less than ten pence sterling a day, he said.

People had a "right to survival at an acceptable level of human existence." In a debate on energy, India criticized the United States for what delegate V. B. Raju termed its profligate use of energy resources. He said he was concerned with the wasteful use of energy for luxury purposes.

Franco improves but still grave

MADRID, Oct. 29 (Reuters): The condition of General Francisco Franco, Spain's 82-year-old Chief of State, improved in the last 24 hours but remained grave, a medical bulletin said tonight.

Franco, whose authoritarian rule has spanned four decades, maintained a normal level of consciousness and muttered weakly to his doctors and family.

Move to aid poorest nations . . .

UK CHANGING FOREIGN AID PRIORITY

BRITAIN ANNOUNCED today that it is changing the priority of its overseas aid in an attempt to help the world's poorest countries – those where people earn on average less than 90 pounds ($180) a year.

These are countries, mainly in Southeast Asia and Africa, which were worst hit by the rise in oil prices but did not benefit from the boom in commodity prices, the Labour Government said in a White Paper.

Britain's overseas aid programme at the moment runs at more than 470 million pounds a year.

Present commitments will be kept up, but the future planning will gradually turn Britain's technical help and consultancy work away from more sophisticated schemes to those having the most direct effect on living and consumption standards in the Third World, informed sources said.

Bleak prospects

The White Paper said nearly 1,000 million people, almost a third of the world population, lived in poor nations whose prospects were "bleak" because they could not attract capital or afford to borrow.

Even if the industrialized countries resumed normal economic growth, the poorest countries were unlikely to benefit by more than about one per cent each year, the document said.

The Government said it would give increasing advances to bilateral aid for the poorest nations and try to set up situations where British funds may stimulate contributions from other Governments.

Although the bulk of total aid would have to come from the oil rich countries, said the document, Britain was ready to cooperate with the Middle East oil producers in giving direct aid to developing countries and was seeking ways of helping with planning projects linked with capital provided by Arab funds.

The document also said Britain's aid should give high priority to efforts to curb population growth.

Cooke off to US Monday

Education Minister the Hon. Howard Cooke, leaves on Monday to fulfill speaking engagements in the United States, as a guest of the Western Carolina University.

He returns on November 6. – API

Extra maize

WASHINGTON, Oct. 29 (Reuters): The United States has sold an additional 400,000 tons of maize to the Soviet Union for shipment this season, the Agriculture Department announced today.

Look for "The Uptown Downtown Shopping Feature" in tomorrow's Gleaner

Mandeville Hospital incident . . .

CORONER TO GET REPORT ON HANGING OF BABY

AN ACCIDENT REPORT on the death of a baby in the Mandeville Hospital last week is to be forwarded to a coroner, the Minister of Health the Hon. Dr. Kenneth McNeill told the House of Representatives yesterday.

The baby's death came to public notice when Councillor Cecil Charlton, Mayor of Mandeville, telegraphed the Prime Minister on Tuesday reporting that the baby fell between the rail and mattress of a crib and died by hanging.

Following is the Minister's statement to Parliament:

"On the night of the 18th October, 1975 an unknown child was brought to the Mandeville Hospital for protection and care. The child was admitted for custody. During the night of October 21, the child was found dead in the crib.

"On Tuesday 28th October the death was reported to the Police by the Matron of the Hospital in consultation with the Hospital Administrator. The child has now been identified. A comprehensive accident report is now being compiled and will be forwarded to the Coroner.

Complaints

"Over the last five years there have been repeated complaints about the quality of patient care at the Mandeville hospital. In response to this, my Ministry has upgraded the staffing and facilities at this Hospital over the last tyree years as follows.

"In 1972 there were five Government medical officers of whom one was a specialist. At present there are seven medical officers of whom three are specialists. In addition at present there are six private medical practicioners who do sessional duty at the hospital.

"During the year 1972 to 1975, the medical man-hours at the hospital have trebled.

"In respect of nursing staff, the number of staff nurses and assistant nurses has nearly doubled since 1972. In the area of administration, the post of Matron has been upgraded from Grade III to Grade IV, and the post of hospital secretary upgraded to hospital administrator.

"Both posts are filled with suitably qualified and experienced staff. Total nursing

(Cont'd on Page 20)

Student held

SACRAMENTO, Oct. 29 (Reuters): Secret Service agents said today they had arrested 32-year-old university student Thomas Tillman on a charge of threatening the life of President Ford last night.

Sale blocked

THE HAGUE, Oct. 29 (Reuters): The Dutch Government has blocked the possible sale to Chile of a new version of the Dutch-built Fokker F-27 Friendship aircraft, an Economics Ministry spokesman said here tonight.

1975

Cindy Breakspeare Wins Miss World Title

1976

The Sunday Gleaner, Section A, December 5, 1976.

TRIUMPHANT CINDY BREAKSPEARE after her crowning as Miss World.

All agog over Cindy

The day after she won the Miss World title, the face of Cindy Breakspeare appeared in every London daily newspaper and in most of the provincial dailies.

The winning of the title by this Jamaican girl has attracted infinitely more publicity, and stories about her have been given ten times as much prominence in the foreign press, than any reports of violence in Jamaica.

Even the conservative **London Times** published a picture of Cindy in a tee-shirt bearing her own portrait, sipping a cup of coffee, and headlined the story – **Jamaica Embarrassed by Its Own Beauty**".

The story, date-lined Kingston, Jamaica, says the official reaction in Jamaica to Cindy's victory was 'one of embarrassment' and pointed out that the government of Jamaica had issued a statement saying it was powerless to order Miss Breakspeare not to take part in the contest, even though South Africa was competing

Other popular dailies concentrated on Cindy's relationship with reggae star Bob Marley and **The Sun** asked "Will Miss World Marry the Prince of Wales?"

Cindy was reported in **The Sun** as saying 'I really want to get married and have at least seven children, but this is the opportunity of a lifetime and I can wait a while Bob has never objected to me entering beauty contests and I think he will be happy for me".

The Sun printed a picture of Cindy looking cool, calm and collected while facing a barrage of a dozen cameramen from the world publications

Top of the world

The Daily Mail said in large type – "Cindy Is Feeling On Top of the World!" and printed a picture of her shortly after her coronation

The mass circulation tabloid **Daily Mirror** said simply, in letters three inches high – "CINDY, OH CINDY!" and followed with a story saying she had "set the world on fire"

The Daily Express reported "It's One in the Eye from Miss Jamaica" and printed a picture of Cindy wearing her crown and winking. The story reported that Miss Jamaica had been urged by her government to quit the contest and disowned by them afterwards.

The Glasgow Sunday Mail published a coloured picture of Cindy in her robes and crown and called her – "The Girl With The World At Her Feet

The London Evening Standard said"Cindy Bubbles Over" and in a special weekend issue the **Daily Mail** printed an interview with Cindy in their column Femail

Cindy posed for the newspaper's photographer in a sexy satin nightgown and the article which included three pictures of Bob Marley was headed, "Miss World and Loving It".

Many of the British newspapers published stories on Cindy for two or three days in succession with pictures taken by their own photographers. In the **Sunday People** she was photographed in a track suit using gymnasium equipment

Cindy was privately sponsored by Ammars Ltd and Air Jamaica After she won the Miss Universe Bikini title in London in September she received a personal invitation from MECCA to take part in the Miss World contest.

In 1975 the Jamaican Government decided that there would be no further official participation in the Miss World contest The MECCA franchise in Jamaica had been held by the Festival Commission but it was decided not to enter again after the last Miss Jamaica, Miss Andrew Lyon, returned from London in 1974 with complaints that blacks girls were discriminated against both by judges of the contest and by the news media

THE EVENING STANDARD reported that the Miss World contest had lost none of its appeal to TV viewers A massive estimated audience of 25 million, the biggest TV audience of the year watched Cindy win the Miss World title

A massive estimated audience of 25 million, the biggest TV audience of the year watched Cindy win the Miss World title.

Good times and ting

The Daily Gleaner

ting JAMAICA'S GOLD MEDAL GRAPEFRUIT DRINK

ESTABLISHED 1834 Price: TWENTY-FIVE CENTS

Vol. CXLIV No. 94 KINGSTON, JAMAICA, MONDAY, APRIL 24, 1978 FOURTEEN PAGES

Ethiopians in new bid to end opposition

NAIROBI, April 23, (Reuter-CANA)

ETHIOPIA'S MARXIST military rulers after the "Red Terror" killings of political opponents in December and January, have embarked on a new phase of their campaign to eliminate opposition — denunciation sessions

Travellers from the Ethiopian capital who reached here today gave the first eyewitness accounts of a new purge which started two weeks ago. It is aimed at the old imperial bureaucracy — ministries, banks and other government institutions — which have so far been little changed by the four-year-old revolution.

According to the eyewitnesses the first mass exposure meeting involved 2,000 employees of the Agriculture Ministry.

They were summoned to the National Theatre in central Addis Ababa for a meeting which lasted from 0830 until dusk. Only pregnant women were allowed out to relieve themselves.

Supervising the meeting were political cadres and kebelle officials. The cadres are officers assigned to look after the political interests of large institutions. Six thousand have so far been trained.

The kebelles are armed groups which have taken over control of local government in Addis Ababa and other towns. They personally round-up and execute anti-government forces.

According to the reports, fear-wracked meeting started with an announcement that the organizers had already drawn up a list of those guilty of sympathizing with opposition groups.

It was announced that the guilty would have the chance to denounce themselves but if they did not, and were exposed by others, they would be shot.

Several ex-members of the main opposition group, the Ethiopian People's Revolutionary Party (EPRP), took the stage and told how they had been saved and allowed to re-enter normal life.

The witnesses said most of these people appeared to be former students.

Then the organizers, acting like cheerleaders, chanted "come on out, come on out" to a rhythmic clapping. One eye witness said they shouted at anyone not clapping: "we see you, we know why you aren't clapping. We know why you are scratching your head".

At the end of the day, 150 people had denounced themselves and gone onto the stage. Another 50 who were exposed by the cadres and kebelle officials were made to sit in two front rows reserved for them.

SCHOOL WORKERS CLAIM TOO

The BITU has asked the Minister of Labour, the Hon. William Isaacs, to intervene in the dispute with the Schools and Colleges Labour Relations Council, over claims for improved wages and fringe benefits for the ancillary staff of the Corporate Area's schools and colleges.

The claims were made in October 1976 to be effective from that year. They include a call for the establishment of a $50-a-week minimum wage, a general increase of $20 per week, pensionable status for all workers, a "proper" medical scheme and improvement in the severance pay arrangements.

Several meetings at the Ministry of Labour since the claims were filed have failed to reach a settlement.

PEACE AND LOVE: Bob Marley gestures as he belts out one of his songs on Saturday night's show along with the I Threes. Below Prime Minister Michael Manley, Mrs. Manley and daughter, Natasha arrive for the show, as also Opposition Leader Mr. Edward Seaga and Tivoli Gardens Councillor, Mr. Desmond McKenzie.

25,000 AT PEACE CONCERT

PM, Seaga join hands and dance

PRIME MINISTER Michael Manley and Opposition Leader Edward Seaga locked hands and danced a short jig, as the curtain went down on Saturday night's "One Love" concert, in aid of the peace efforts, at the National Stadium.

A full moon, dodging between patches of dark clouds, dangled overhead as some 25,000 people including the two political leaders, Minister of National Security Senator Dudley Thompson and his Opposition rival, Senator Winston Spaulding, were treated to a marathon trouble-free show climaxing with the performance of international reggae star Bob Marley.

Superstar Marley was close to the end of his 45 minute performance when he requested Mr. Manley and Mr. Seaga to join him on stage.

It was Mr. Seaga who got up first. He walked to the ten-foot high stage, held out his arms and was hauled up by peace initiator Claudius Massop and a stage hand.

A few minutes later Mr. Manley joined the Opposition Leader on stage. Bob told them to shake hands, they gave a firm handshake, before gripping Bob's hand, and all three held up for the crowd to see a pyramid shaped grip of hands, as Bob belted out the show's theme song "One Love".

Tosh lashes out

A Rastafarian ran onstage with a lighted chillum pipe used in smoking ganja, and started passing it around to the dozens of people who had joined them. Senator Thompson watched the proceedings from his reserved seat. After the song ended Mr. Seaga and Mr. Manley walked in different directions to their seats.

Just 90 minutes before, a former member of Bob's group

(Cont'd. on Page 11 Col. 1)

Inside Story

- Latest on Teachers strike ... Page 2
- Pay restraint .... Page 3
- St. Anne's student at UNESCO .... Page 5
- Guest column .... Page 6
- Gomes, Phillip win .... Page 8
- What abortion means .... Page 12

1978

Born in Jamaica: A Symbol of Caribbean Pride

Minna Israel

Every great achievement is a dream before it becomes a reality, and the vision of The University of the West Indies (The UWI) was about excelling, having a deep understanding of the requirements of its society and its needs, given our history. The British influence on society is well established. The Caribbean as a region, battled forces of imperialism for centuries, that left a legacy of poverty, illiteracy, dependency, and absentee governance. Independence brought a deep desire to explore the inequalities in a variety of institutions and practices that can be located in meanings and beliefs in our society at the time.

It was our good fortune here in Jamaica, to be chosen as the founding campus when this academy was birthed in 1948, as a university college of London with 33 medical students. Today, The UWI's five campuses and 10 global centres represent a symbol of success for the Caribbean Community, and Jamaica has also become the proud location of its regional headquarters.

World-class tertiary education exists right here at home. Since 2018, our UWI has been consistently ranked among the top universities globally by the most reputable ranking agency, Times Higher Education (THE), standing among the top 1.5 per cent of the global pool. We are the only Caribbean university to make these prestigious ranking lists, and we are also featured among the leading universities for its response to the world's biggest concerns, outlined in the 17 United Nations Sustainable Development Goals (SDGs).

The UWI has changed the way the world views the region and continues to be a pivotal force in every aspect of Caribbean development to improve the well-being of people across the region. As a university with social justice as part of its core mission, our academy established the Centre for Gender and Development Studies in 1993, with teaching and research focused on mainstreaming gender into development planning, programming and policy implementation to reform development practice and laws towards more equitable and sustainable outcomes. And in 2019, The UWI ushered in a new era in the global reparations movement.

Leading as an activist university, from social justice to climate justice, our regional university serves as the global leader mobilising the International Association of Universities' Global University Consortium on SDG 13 (Climate Action). For decades our scientists have made research contributions on climate change and sustainable development that impact the world, landing The UWI recognition as a leading university producer of information on Small Island Developing States. More recently, The UWI climate change research and modelling informed The '1.5 to Stay Alive' Caribbean campaign aimed at mobilising the global effort to limit global warming to 1.5 degrees above pre-industrial levels, and avoid the catastrophic effects of climate change.

The UWI's legacy is over seven decades of service and leadership across the region and the wider world. Beyond teaching, research, and the production of knowledge, we've gone a step further to prioritise building global partnerships and connecting knowledge to opportunities for multi-stakeholder development solutions. Our global footprint is extended through the contributions of an annual average of 3000+ alumni. Among these include Emmy Award and Man Booker Prize to Nobel Prize winners, CEOs to entrepreneurs, academics to artists, leaders of Caribbean nations to leaders across all sectors, impacting the globe at the forefront of their fields, and over 25 have risen to become heads of government or heads of state within the Caribbean.

Over the decades, The UWI has also nurtured sporting talent who have achieved international success including star cricketers and track and field athletes. The university's quest to be a centre of sporting excellence came into focus when The UWI Faculty of Sport was officially launched in July 2017. At the 2020 Tokyo Summer Games, UWI students and alumni shone with four Olympic medals won by Jamaican competitors who were Pelicans from the Mona campus.

The UWI has been our lighthouse, to leave behind poverty, illiteracy and embrace our arts, culture, and social services, natural products, and pioneer medicine and climate science. As an institution it has evolved into an internationally respected academy, a post-colonial light, guiding us along a pathway to development since Independence, giving every Jamaican an opportunity to have a stake in this country and its future. Thinking about the future of education would be an exercise of imagination had it not been for The UWI which made possible, what might otherwise seem unthinkable. The UWI has answered the 'call' to support our people to achieve their best.

The difficulties and obstacles can all be positive blessings, as they knit the muscles more firmly and teach us self-reliance.

Over the past 60 years, my country, Jamaica, gave me schooling, independence of action and opportunity for service.

> *"I am indebted to my country beyond any human power to repay." (Herbert Hoover)*

Happy, Safe & Prosperous 60th Birthday!

Minna Israel is a retired financial services executive; a past president of the International Women's Forum, Jamaica Chapter; a Rotarian; a Fundraiser; and experienced corporate director, presently serving on a number of Boards including First Global Bank, RJRGLEANER Communications Group, Carimed Group, Stanley Motta Limited, and Jamaica Public Service Co.

Resilience: The Source of Our Greatness

Patrick Hylton

I was born and raised in Four Paths, Clarendon. I am the son of an educator, whose lessons for me transcended what I needed in the classroom.

One of my earliest memories were the little pieces of paper with quotes and inspirational messages she would pack in my lunch bag each day. Many of those quotes would strengthen me on challenging days, and there were many. Little did I know, she was planting seeds, watering the roots, and fostering what I believe most embodies my fellow Jamaicans, our RESILIENCE.

To many across the world, Jamaicans are the greatest to ever live and the best to ever do things. It is impossible to deny the prowess of our world-leading, world-beating athletes, the impact our music has on billions of people, and the world-best product that is our tourism. There are many of us that are not as famous, but no less prominent or dominant in our chosen fields. In 2021, two Jamaicans were named among *Forbes'* CEO Next list, which recognised 50 business leaders and executives who are leading candidates in line to run some of America's most respected companies. We accounted for four per cent of the list, while our population is less than one per cent of the US population. We can point to countless such success stories of first and second generation Jamaicans.

But, we don't have to look beyond our shores to find amazing Jamaicans. Greatness emanates within our borders. In 2022, Rear Admiral Antonette Wemyss-Gorman became the first woman chief of defence staff for the Jamaica Defence Force. In 2018, the Jamaica Stock Exchange was recognised as the top performing stock exchange in the world. Yet, what lies below the surface and what many eyes did not see is the magnitude of challenges overcome to achieve such greatness. The secret behind our undisputed greatness is not excess talent, but rather abundant resilience. We rise in spite of poverty, discrimination, misogyny, personal trauma and countless challenges. It is something we should celebrate, even as we work toward mitigating these challenges.

Over the years in my chosen field, I have had the opportunity to meet with leaders and sit on boards in other countries with stronger economies. These leaders often struggle to adapt during recessions or periods of volatility. Yet, every leader in the Jamaican context only knows how to operate with constraints, and so we are never daunted during tough times. *Tun yuh han mek fashion* is the norm. It is this resilience that enabled us to have successfully navigated the debt restructuring programme with the International Monetary Fund (IMF), while other countries were unable to stave off default. We were resolute in our refusal to default on international monetary obligations and this galvanised a coalition of Government and Opposition, public and private sectors and civilian society, united in our commitment to not fail. Today, the model for countries in tough economic situations, especially the debt restructuring programmes of the International Monetary Fund, is Jamaica.

As the World Bank detailed in the country's context explanation:

> *In 2013, Jamaica launched an ambitious reform programme to stabilise the economy, reduce debt, and fuel growth, gaining national and international support.*

Public debt fell below 100 per cent of GDP in 2018/19 from a high of close to 150 per cent in 2013 and is expected to decline below 60 per cent by 2025/26, in line with the provisions of the Fiscal Responsibility Law. The rate of unemployment also fell to a historic low of 7.2 per cent in October 2019, which is almost half the rate at the start of the reform programme.

We have shown a phenomenal macroeconomic turnaround, from a crippling debt environment to positive economic growth for 20 consecutive quarters , up to the onset of the novel Coronavirus pandemic on our shores in March 2020.

The experience in all can be summarised by the Latin proverb, *The brave may fall, but never yield.*

Cup Runneth Over ...

Today, I stand on the shoulders of Mrs Tekla Hylton, a great woman who spent all her adult years moulding the minds of primary-school children in York Town, Clarendon. Many still contact me today to share the impact she had on their lives. She poured into me, my three siblings, and thousands of other children for well over 40 years, preparing us to rise in spite of challenges.

Today, I have the privilege of leading the NCB Financial Group, an institution celebrating its 185th anniversary, having overcome many of its own challenges. Yet still, we have helped thousands of customers to unlock their dreams and attain their goals. We have helped over 100,000 people through the donations of the NCB. Foundation and we have generated wealth for thousands of shareholders.

On our 'Rock' of 4,244 square miles resilience is pervasive. Our children are fed an intrinsic belief in self, *likkle but wi tallawah'.* For a little dot in the sea, who has had more impact?

As we elebrate 60 years of Independence, I celebrate our resilience and all we have accomplished as a nation, and as a people. Let us continue to nurture this resilience because that will allow us to weather any storm. It is our competitive advantage.

However, let us also take the lessons from our greatest successes and apply those to the significant challenges and social ills that continue to plague us. Let us become galvanised as one in the same way we stood together during our greatest test with the IMF agreement.

The power of our combined resilience will put us on an accelerated path to Vision 2030, making Jamaica, the indisputable place of choice to live, work, raise families and do business.

Patrick Hylton is President & CEO of NCB Financial Group Limited.

JAMAICA 60 – To the World and Beyond!

Sanjay Lewis

Rise Up! Stand and take your place, shine like the sun, your journey has just begun!
Rise up! Stand like the brave, rule your destiny ... be the best that you can be!

It was in the year of our Lord, 1997, when our little island home Jamaica qualified for the very first, and only, time to be part of the big boys' club and play on the big stage, as part of the FIFA World Cup, dubbed that year as *'The Road to France'.*

What a journey it was! We were finally realizing our World Cup dream, and the hopes of an entire nation of black, green, and gold patriots lay firmly, or maybe even rested heavily on the backs of the squad. It's hard not to pen this article in a poetic style, because one can easily say that history was made on Sunday, November 16, 1997 as united shouts of thrill and acclamation reverberated through the city of Kingston into the hills of St. Andrew, echoing from coast to coast and straight through the heart of the diaspora.

That final qualifier at the National Stadium was a moment that remains etched in the minds of so many people and is definitely one that will quite likely, never be forgotten. Nil–all! was the score ... Yes O–O, believe it or not ... but that was all that we needed to make the cut. Onward to France we all went, beaming with pride, our heads lifted high! The support of every single Jamaican at home and abroad throughout the entire journey to qualification will never be forgotten. For one, it showed us all, that in spite of our differences in background, education, denomination or political affiliation, we can rally together seamlessly in support of a cause we all believe in, a mission that places our little rock centrestage in world affairs.

The original Reggae Boyz team, players like Warren Barrett, Onandi Lowe, Deon Burton, Ian 'Pepe' Goodison, Theodore Whitmore, and Winston Griffiths, blazed a trail of excellence, as cliché as that sounds, a trail that might very well remain unmatched for several more years ... only time will tell. Their dedication, passion and tenacity showed

Jamaicans from all walks of life, that in spite of our many difficulties, our setbacks and the challenges we face as a developing nation, Jamaica is truly blessed and has really made impressive strides in a relatively short lifespan. This little dot in the middle of the Caribbean Sea between North and South America will always show up, stand strong and as the young ones say now-a-days, 'Slay'!

I certainly think that what our World-Cup-qualifying moment that year really highlighted is that there are, by far, more things that join us together than there are things that separate us. That historic moment really set the stage for the sporting world to take notice of 'Jamrock' ... an island nation that would later become known as the 'sprint factory' that produces some of the world's greatest runners: Merlene Ottey, Juliet Cuthbert, Dion Hemmings, Brigitte Foster Hylton, Delloreen Ennis London, Veronica Campbell Brown, Shelly-Ann Fraser Pryce, Elaine Thompson-Herah, Kerron Stewart, Sherone Simpson, Usain Bolt, Asafa Powell, Yohan Blake, Nesta Carter, Michael Frater, Hansle Parchment, and many, many more.

Jamaica's contribution to the world is rich; our culture is vibrant and we are truly Out of Many, One People!

As we celebrate the BIG-60 and look ahead to another 60, let us use this moment to remember how proud we are to be Jamaican, to stand true to our national pledge that encourages us to work diligently and creatively, to think generously and honestly… so that Jamaica may, under God, increase in beauty, fellowship and prosperity, and play her part in advancing the welfare of the whole human race.

RISE UP Jamaica!

Sanjay Lewis is a co-host on the Morning Agenda on Power 106FM and an adjunct lecturer in Introduction to Politics at University of the Commonwealth Caribbean.

ROOTED IN RESILIENCE AND BOLDNESS – JNCB

Given the impact Jamaica has had on the world stage, there's no denying we are used to punching above our weight class. The past 60 years have seen us tested by time and tried by challenges, but surviving and growing in spite of it all. Becoming who we are, in fact, because of it all. From the far-reaching influence of our music to the contributions of our National Heroes, and the achievements of our athletes, our presence has been felt across the globe.

The same tenacity, creativity and confidence that have origins in our ancestry run through the veins of today's unsung heroes, Jamaicans achieving greatness in their respective corners of life. The boldness and resilience born in our forebears and forged in the fires of time are evident today in the lesser-known, but meaningful achievements of our teachers, doctors, nurses, and other Jamaicans doing what they can every day to realize their visions.

In 2018, the Jamaica Stock Exchange was recognised as the top-performing stock exchange in the world. In 2021, two Jamaicans were named on *Forbes* Magazine's 'CEO Next' list, which recognised 50 business leaders in line to run America's most successful companies. This year, Rear Admiral Antonette Wemyss Gorman became the first woman chief of defence staff for the Jamaica Defence Force. Our sprinters dominate international competition, with our women occupying two out of the three top-fastest spots, and our men holding three of the four fastest times in their category.

However, what lies beneath the surface, and what many eyes did not see, are the challenges overcome to achieve such greatness. The secret behind our greatness is about more than talent, but rather an abundance of resilience. We rise despite countless hurdles. Our resilience is something to be celebrated, even as we continue to face challenges head on.

Jamaican resilience and bold aspirations led to the inception and growth of the National Commercial Bank Jamaica Limited (NCB), now the largest financial institution in Jamaica. NCB has faced challenges along the journey and has persevered through economic downturns and the Jamaica Debt Exchange to becoming Jamaica's top financial institution. And the entity has continued to grow, becoming a key part of the NCB Financial Group, with a presence in over 21 territories in the region.

With roots going back 185 years, NCB has always been a part of Jamaica's history. In 1837 the Colonial Bank of London, England opened its doors on Harbour Street. Through a series of mergers and acquisitions, the bank became Barclays Bank of Jamaica Limited and eventually emerged in August 1977 as National Commercial Bank Jamaica Limited, now a part of a leading financial conglomerate in the Caribbean. The NCB story is a homage to the customers and employees, who have been the most important part of the journey, and to the Jamaican spirit behind the organisation's mission.

The boldness of NCB's legacy can be seen in the continuous introduction of world-class innovations to the marketplace. NCB introduced the first Jamaican credit card. NCB was first to bring automated banking machines (ABMs) and, more recently, intelligent ABMs to the island. NCB also played a part in the launch of the first digital wallet to accommodate JAMDEX, Jamaica's historic Central Bank Digital Currency.

While NCB has developed resilience over the years, the company continues to inspire resilience by 'building a better Jamaica' by empowering Jamaicans, moving its people and their ideas from ambition to achievement. Through charitable initiatives, the NCB Foundation has donated more than $2 billion to provide over 250,000 Jamaicans with valuable tools, including access to education. The Foundation is also playing a pivotal role in accelerating the digital transformation of Jamaica by expanding the country's pool of digital producers through the provision of tertiary scholarships and grants.

As we continue to strive for greatness as a country, NCB is here for it. Rooted in resilience and driven by a passion for excellence, remaining boldly committed to fulfilling the purpose of empowering people. Unlocking dreams. Building communities.

Congratulations 'Jamaica, land we love', on your diamond anniversary of Independence.

The National Commercial Bank branch in New Kingston, displaying its new monogram, NCB, on its façade in February 1978. It was one of the former branches of Barclays Bank.

TOP L-R: **Dean Simpson** - Head - NCB Financial Centre, Fairview, **Lloyd Richardson** - Head - NCB Financial Centre, Mandeville **Brian Baggoo** - Head - NCB Financial Centre, St. Ann's Bay **BOTTOM L-R:** **Laurie Spencer** - Head - NCB Financial Centre, May Pen, **Wayne Hunter** - Head - NCB Financial Centre, Duke Street, **Maxine McKenzie** - Head - NCB Financial Centre, Constant Spring

Empowering people. Unlocking dreams.
Building communities.

NATIONAL COMMERCIAL BANK JAMAICA LIMITED
185 YEARS

The Daily Gleaner

50 CENTS
Vol. CXLVII No. 104 ESTABLISHED 1834 KINGSTON, JAMAICA, SATURDAY, MAY 2, 1981 TWENTY PAGES

ROHM & HAAS
TOK Selective Weed Killer
DITHANE M-45 Fungicide
GEDDES GRANT

CEREMONIAL MARKS GRANT OF CITY STATUS

Montego Bay comes into its own

MAYOR SEES NEW ECONOMIC AND SOCIAL CHALLENGE

From KEN ALLEN, Associate Editor

MONTEGO BAY, May 1:

WITH THE BOOM OF GUNS and martial music, this North Coast town was formally proclaimed the City of Montego Bay at 11.15 a.m. today.

In a festive 90-minute ceremonial, the Minister of Local Government, the Hon. Pearnel Charles, read the formal proclamation according the town "the title, style, recognition privileges and status of a city."

Thousands packed historic Sam Sharpe Square, a-flutter with flags and bunting, brilliant in the morning sunshine, and buzzing with excitement at the re-birth of a city – which it was, before the upheaval of the Morant Bay Rebellion removed that status in 1865.

The salute to city status was led by Governor-General, the Most Hon. Sir Florizel Glaspole, who declared his pride in having given assent to the Parliamentary Act which gave city status to Montego Bay on October 9, 1980.

Sir Florizel also led the exhortations which marked the oratory of the occasion.

"Your city status creates a new dimension of both width and depth and the first necessary step is for each and every one to develop a deep sense of pride for belonging to the City of Montego Bay," Sir Florizel said.

Earlier, a message from Prime Minister, the Hon. Edward Seaga, was read by the Minister of Health, Dr. Kenneth Baugh. The Prime Minister said, inter alia:

"The new status presents a challenge to the people of Montego Bay to continue the building of their city to a higher pedestal and to strengthen the base for social and economic progress. I have no doubt about their capacity to do this for they have always shown themselves to be productive people..."

The Minister of Local Government added his quota: "It is a time of celebration, but it is also a time to sit down and plan for the future, to use your imagination and initiative to continue to build and to ensure that you live up to the great honour which has been conferred on you today. This is not the end of the struggle, it is merely the beginning..."

More pragmatic than ceremonial, Mayor Shallman Scott declared that Montego Bay could no longer be called a "Second City" to Kingston, but a city holding its own status and demanding an end to "the historical problem of centralised bureaucracy" which deprived it of key government and social agencies.

"Today, May 1", he said,"presents a new challenge to us here in Sam Sharpe Square, in Montego Bay, in St. James,

(Cont'd. on Page 17 Col. 4)

MONTEGO BAY'S BIG DAY: Highlights of yesterday's ceremonial marking the conferring of city status on Montego Bay. At left, the Minister of Local Government, the Hon. Pearnel Charles, reads the proclamation as the Mayor of the city, Councillor Shallman Scott, listens. At right, the new Custos of St. James takes the Oath of Office being administered to him by the Governor-General, Sir Florizel Glasspole.

Dog racing as tourist attraction?

MONTEGO BAY, May 1

Mayor Shallman Scott announced here today that this new city is examining the possibility of establishing the sport of dog-racing as a tourist attraction as well as for economic benefit.

The announcement was one of the pragmatic aspects of today's ceremonial salute to city status for Montego Bay.

Other news came from Local Government Minister, the Hon. Pearnel Charles, who said that as practical gifts to celebrate the day, the new city will get two water trucks to ease periods of drought and a new garbage unit to help keep the city clean.

Mr. Charles said that although he was from the east he had brought "no gold, frankincense or myrrh"; but he would give as gifts from the Ministry of Finance the two water trucks and the garbage unit.

The announcement about the water trucks brought cheers from the crowd, keenly aware of perennial problems of water shortage in Montego Bay.

The Minister also promised new fire-fighting equipment at a time to be negotiated.

In his speech, Mayor Scott laid stress on "the practical level".

"We have already identified a suitable location for street vendors, so that the streets may once again be clear and clean. We are in discussion with owners of property in Red Hills to create a botanical garden and children's park.

"We have asked the Government to declare Montego Freeport a free zone area for the purpose of attracting more investment, which will generate more employment.

"We have asked the Montego Bay Development Committee, in conjunction with the Parks and Gardens Committee, chaired by Councillor Dockey Cunningham, to take charge of the beautification of the city.

"And we are looking at the possibility of having dog-racing in Montego Bay which can provide not only a popular sport for tourist and locals but also generate income for the improvement of our social infrastructure", the Mayor said.

– KEN ALLEN

Jamaica Meat Packers to be phased out

JAMAICA MEAT PACKERS LIMITED, which was formed in November 1976 to "offset an imminent pig glut situation" and which up to mid-April had a total indebtedness of $891,972, is to be phased out over the next three months.

This decision was announced by the Minsiter of Agriculture, the Hon. Percival Broderick, to representatives of the Jamaica Livestock Association's Pig Committee, as well as pig farmers and meat packers, as an attempt to solve the current problems facing the pig industry.

Dr. Broderick told to the meeting, which was held on Tuesday, that in August 1980, a study of J.M.P. was made by an official audit team which found that J.M.P. could not become a viable company "even if existing debts are written off and maximum efficiency is achieved" and recommended to the then Government that the company be closed.

The mid-April indebtedness of J.M.P. includes payment of deficit on operations and outstanding debts to commercial banks.

DEFICIT

It is anticipated, the meeting was told, that the payment of deficit on operations for the next three months to cover purchase and sale of an anticipated 3,600 pi gs will be $85,284, bringing the indebtedness to $977,256. The value of the inventory of J.M.P. over the same period was $355,051.

Dr. Broderick told the meeting that once more a glut situation was imminent. Pork production is now exceeding the requirements of the processors and

(Cont'd. on Page 17 Col. 7)

... Montego Bay could no longer be called a "Second City" to Kingston, but a city holding its own status ...

Leading citizens of Montego Bay and other distinguished guests on the platform in Sam Sharpe Square on City Status Day on Friday, May 1, 1981. Sharing in the proud occasion (fourth from right) is Dr. Kenneth Baugh, Minister of Health, the Member for Parliament for North West St. James.

The march past of Boy Scouts and Girl Guides during the ceremony granting city status to Montego Bay on Friday, May 1, 1981.

1981

THE DAILY GLEANER, THURSDAY, AUGUST 26, 1982 PAGE ELEVEN

P.M. SPELLS OUT ASPECTS OF H.E.A.R.T. PROGRAMME

'Meaningful assault on vocational training'

Continued from Page 1

programme, involving garments skills, school-leavers, youth corps, youth camps and craft training in community centres; a $4.4 million agricultural skills training programme in the Ministry of Agriculture, and a $2.8 million programme in the Ministry of Industry and Commerce.

However lack of co-ordination and proper direction of the programmes had resulted in duplication and poor direction.

DIRECTION AND DRIVE

Against this background, the Government took the decision to establish HEART as the co-ordinating mechanism to give "direction and drive" to the national skills training programme

HEART would devise training programmes to suit the needs of the available jobs; streamline existing programmes to make them more job-oriented or directed to self-employment; monitor training with active field supervisors; and finance the projects.

Financing would come from Budgetary allocation, which this year was $12 million; multi-lateral and bi-lateral skills projects, including a $30-million U.S. A.I.D. programme being negotiated; as well as the funds already allocated to various Ministries, including the Ministeries of Agriculture, Industry and Commerce and Youth, for similar training

HEART would also offer assistance in employment opportunities by providing a job-placement service for graduates, and establish a placement desk for skilled Jamaicans overseas who wished to return home to work.

Capital financing for self-employment projects including oyster-cultivation, bee-farming, small-stock rearing and cottage industries, would also be provided.

The training programme was to be closely monitored with the service of active field supervisors to ensure that once the projects were in place they pursued set directions

FACTORY

In the industrial skills sector, a new programme was to come on stream this year in garments, sewn and knitted products.

A complex is to be established at Marcus Garvey Drive in Kingston to accommodate in the first instance 20 factories each employing 250 persons, or a total of 5,000 employees over the first five years

Marcus Garvey Drive was selected because of the need for a school for the training programme, and the Sites and Service project at Marcus Garvey Drive already had infrastructure including roads and plumbing, and walls already being put up, as well as the fact that it was in an highly-industralized area.

The Ministry of Industry and Commerce was finalizing arrangements with a foreign source to finance the building of the 20 factories on a prefabricated basis.

Craft skills training would involve work in straw, wood, pewter, embroidery and ceramics.

Speaking on the School Leavers Programme which is to start in early October, Mr. Seaga said the programme was open to graduates who have achieved three G C.E. passes or four J.S.C. passes

In Year One of the programme, the selected persons would receive $50 weekly and the employers will be able to write off that amount against profits. In the second and third years, the employers will be offered tax credits of 75% for males and 80% for females.

FIRMS AND SCHOOLS

Firms with wage bills of $86,600 annually or $7,222 per month, are involved.

The list of firms has already been selected from National Housing Trust computer lists and circularized These firms have been sent a brochure explaining the programme as well as a registration form.

Mr Seaga said that 1,162 firms had been circularised. Response had already been received from 73 firms, totalling 364 trainees out of the quota which had been allotted them of 395.

However, 73 firms were "a very small percentage" of the total number, and there was a need for firms who have not yet responded to respond promptly

Some of the firms had indicated that they would accept more than their quota and he advised that firms which took more than their quotas would get additional benefits.

The schools have also been circularized to provide the 4,000 trainees required for this year. Applications have been approved for 3,352 trainees of which 2,412 are from the rural areas and 910 from the Corporate Area (1,180 males and 2,172 females).

One of the problems which would be encountered was that of matching up rural trainees with opportunities because of the shortage of industries in the rural areas

SPECIAL TRAINING

Alternative programmes would have to be worked out and it was proposed to tackle the problem in two ways: (i) a programme of continuing education, using post-Primary institutions and teachers to bring the trainees to levels sufficient to enter university, CAST, nurse-training or teacher-training institutions; (ii) enrolment in special Ministry of Education programmes in various areas of occupation, which were being designed

In the case of the continuing education programme, the student would not be paid the full $50 as the teachers would also be paid from the amount for the extra services.

One of the projects being designed by the Ministry of Education was called JOBS (Jamaican Opportunities for Business Success) which was a joint venture project with a foreign firm utilising interactive computer programme to accelerate training

Mr. Seaga described the HEART programme as the "most meaningful assault on vocational training the country has witnessed to date"

After fulfilling its initial role of creating the machinery to co-ordinate Government's skills training programme, its next step would be to rescue the "decay" among young people "who are inevitably being consigned to the waste heap."

The skills training programme would involve 10,000 persons in the first year and would be increased to 15,000 per annum with new projects being added

This year's project involves the training of: 1,000 per annum in agricultural skills, 2,200 per annum in building skills, 1,700 per annum in industrial skills; including garments and embroidery; 1,000 per annum in craft skills; and the School Leavers programme with 4,000 per annum.

In addition, the Government proposed to revise the Apprenticeship Training Programme to put in a proper system which would involve a substantial number of persons.

... the Government took the decision to establish HEART ... to give 'direction and drive" to the national skills training programme.

...gramme despite its link with labour.

In the agricultural skills training programme, the Eden Park Scheme in his West Central St Mary constituency was being run on "political basis" and many of the youths involved were not from the immediate area.

He hoped that the Inspectors who would monitor the projects should not become a disincentive to business people and cause them not to be too enamoured with the programme

He asked what would happen after the training was completed and whether those being trained in agricultural skills would be given land to do their own farming.

Dr. Gilmour said that the registration forms sent to schools had attached a choice of areas in which the students would wish to be trained, as well as 28 training areas and each carrying various modules of training

She said 40 children from "deep rural areas" were being used in an experiment on the use of computer-based education which will last for six weeks. With the introduction of computerised education, the country would be able to re-introduce old programmes such as the work experience programme under which people were released from work to go to school.

Dr Gilmour said that, despite the problems, whatever the price her Ministry was determined to make it work, because the suffering of the young people was enough to give the courage to make it succeed.

1982

Jamaica's team did its fastest time, 59.4 seconds … . They outpushed both the United States and West German teams …

KINGSTON, JAMAICA, MONDAY, FEBRUARY 22, 1988

Jamaica's bobsled team does its fastest time

JAMAICA'S team did its fastest time, 59.4 seconds, in the two-man bobsled event at the Calgary Winter Games yesterday.

The team's efforts, which placed them in 16th position after the completing of three heats, were undermined by a Russian protest which forced the abandonment of the final two heats.

Protesting track conditions, Soviet team officials had demanded that the competition be decided on the basis of Saturday's two runs, which would have given the Soviet Union's top competitor the gold medal. Instead, the race jury rescheduled the two final heats for today, when temperatures were expected to dip below freezing. The 1,612-metre (4,838-foot) track's refrigeration unit struggled to offset temperatures near 10 degrees centigrade (50°F) at the start of the race. The course was also covered by wind-blown sand in many spots.

Thirty-one of 41 teams had already completed their heats when the Russian protest came.

Before then, Jamaica's team of driver Dudley Stokes Jnr, and pusher Michael White was in great form. They outpushed both the United States and West German teams, in the process registering the under one minute clocking.

1988

Every Cloud has a Silver Lining

Dr Neil Gardner

On Thursday, September 8, 1988, the seventh named storm of the hurricane season was formed in the eastern Caribbean and given the name 'Gilbert'. Initially, Gilbert did not appear to be a threat to our island, but as the weekend drew to a close, it seemed an ominous and almost certain danger. We have had numerous storms appear to be headed straight for our beautiful isle, only to make a last-minute turn, as if we really were being guarded by the mighty hand of our anthem's Eternal Father. On Monday, September 12, at 10:00 a.m., however, Hurricane Gilbert made landfall on the east coast of Jamaica with the 'eye' travelling east to west along the midline of the island. Gilbert caused an estimated US$4-billion-worth of damage and claimed 45 lives across the island. Losses were racked up from destroyed crops, buildings, roads, and small aircraft, with more than 100,000 houses destroyed or damaged island-wide.

I remember just starting fourth form at Wolmer's Boys' School earlier the previous week and then forced to extend our summer break for a few more weeks as the school was completely destroyed, including, to my dismay, the biology, physics and chemistry labs. If I were to stop here, we would miss out on probably the single greatest story of togetherness, nation-building and civic pride that I have ever experienced. During the storm, a coconut tree fell on to our nextdoor neighbour's roof. The family had recently moved to the community and we had hardly ever spoken. When the eye of the storm arrived, my father and I, while assessing the damage to our home, saw the situation nextdoor and rushed over to their home with machetes in hand and helped them to cut away the tree from their roof before the eye passed. After the hurricane had departed our shores many people were seen walking around the community in groups with machetes and axes, and other implements to assist those who were trapped in their homes. Powerlines were down, trees were levelled and thousands of homes partially or totally destroyed.

In the absence of electricity, children in the community came together every day to spend time with one another. We played football and ring games, rode bicycles, swam and told stories to keep one another entertained. If someone did not have food, those with food would share. Some people owned a generator, colloquially called a 'Delco', and many would help store meat for those who did not have one. Some of the more affluent people in our community, who owned swimming pools, allowed us to collect water from their pools so we could, among other things, wash our clothes and flush our toilets, during the first several weeks after the storm when we had no water. Beyond a community benefit, the disaster seemed a bit of a blessing to me and my burgeoning athletic career.

Later that school year, during the track season, in my second year of class 3 at the Boys' Athletics Championships, I won my first gold medal, equalled the record in the high jump, but injured my ankle in the process. That year, the CARIFTA Games, which normally would have taken place the week after Champs, was postponed for four months to August 1989 because of the devastation in the host country caused by Hurricane Gilbert the previous year. The CARIFTA Games only had two age categories: athletes under 17 and those under 20 years old during the year of competition. The extra time that was afforded to me enabled me to recover from my injury and

continue to grow and get stronger. I was victorious at the CARIFTA trials over athletes two years older than me, which qualified me, at 14 years old to make my very first national team. I would later go on to win the bronze medal at the CARIFTA Games, in the high jump.

I dare not trivialise the negative impact that the hurricane had on our society or on the lives of many individuals across our nation. I do realize that there was a lot of suffering and loss, but as I share, out of something catastrophic came numerous occasions for good. Gilbert to some represented the worst of times, but for many others Gilbert represented the best of times. I was very proud of our little island in the sun and I know that the same drive that brought us together still resides within us all, awaiting the right situation to rekindle the still-flickering flame of our indomitable spirit. I pray that it will not take another catastrophe for us to shine.

As we reflect on the 60 years of our Independent Jamaica, let us seek to fan into flame the passion that burns within us to serve one another and to bring honour and glory to our beloved homeland.

Dr Neil Gardner is a Jamaican Olympian and Chiropractic Neurologist.

The Urban Development Corporation

Dianna Blake-Bennett

There is one institution that transformed my hometown and had the biggest impact on my life, the Urban Development Corporation (UDC).

I am Montegonian, and as those of us from the Second City would say 'born a Bay'. In 1975, my mother, Patricia Blake, went to work with the UDC as a secretary and by 1977 she was promoted to office manager, and so I have an intimate relationship with organisation as she spent the better part of 30 years with the institution. The UDC's office at 40 Fort Street, beside what was then the Jamintel building, was my haunt after school, and where I watched my mother and the team of architects, engineers, draughtsmen and the several project managers from head office in Kingston, transform my then small tourist town of Montego Bay, paving the way for city status in 1981.

The UDC was at the time headed by the late Gloria Knight, small in stature, but who was larger than life, and in my youthfulness someone to be feared. When she was coming from Kingston to the Montego Bay Office, let's say there was increased alacrity. Unknown to me at the time, these two women at the UDC, my mother and Mrs. Knight, would later be my inspiration as in the early 1980s there were few women at the top in large organizations, and deep within me these women planted a seed that would later blossom, driving me to where I am today.

In 1977, the UDC dredged the foreshore, just before Fort Street, creating the Howard Cooke Highway, the Walter Fletcher Beach, 'Dump Up Beach' and several commercial land spaces, which today house the Sagicor Montego Bay Commercial and Bay West shopping centres, as well as the Tax Administration Jamaica Office. The real estate between Dump Up Beach and Walter Fletcher Beach was earmarked for hotel development.

These developments created fervour within the town which was growing and providing economic benefits to all. It resuscitated the township, as no development had taken place since the 1960s.

The opening of the Howard Cooke Highway remains fresh in my memory as there was a huge show at the new amphitheatre and along the highway.

But the changes to the waterfront were just the start; the next major development that I can recall being done by the UDC was the Catherine Hall housing scheme. There were about 300 new housing solutions in the first phase, and again a big excitement as many Montegonians were realising home ownership. This was the 'talk a Bay'. The project went so well that phase two was quick in coming. The now larger community of Catherine Hall required a school, giving birth to the Catherine Hall Primary School.

Walter Fletcher Beach became a second home in my teen years, my hideaway during the summer and on Sundays. There was also a Friday Beach party held weekly that was the kick-off for the weekend in my early 20s.

On my most recent visit home, I passed the Harmony Beach Park (previously Dump Up Beach) and thought 40 years or so later the UDC is still crafting and shaping this stretch along the foreshore, a beautiful well-thought-out recreational space made for us.

In 1968 the UDC was incorporated by an Act of Parliament, with the mandate to be a catalyst of growth in the nation through major infrastructure development.

I celebrate on our 60th anniversary of Independence the work and worth of the UDC for its hand in the transformation of my hometown and my life.

You have lived up to your mantra, Making Development Happen!

Dianna Blake-Bennett is Chief Executive Officer, Manufacturing Division – Jamaican Teas Ltd.

Wi Likkle but Wi Tallawah!

Nicola Madden-Greig, OD

Where do we begin? 'Exodus', the album by Jamaican musical icon Bob Marley became Time *magazine's album of the century in 1999. This tiny island is a dominant force in track and field with record-breaking giants, such as Usain St Leo Bolt, Elaine Thompson-Herah, Shelly-Ann Fraser-Pryce, Asafa Powell, and so many others. This year our country sent an expanded bobsled team to the Winter Olympics, yes the Winter one, clearly not satisfied with only making an impact at the Summer Games. The first time we did that resulted in a movie being made about it.*

Off the radar of international celebrities and legends our tiny island still accomplishes amazing achievements on the international stage. To highlight just a few, Jamaican writer Marlon James won the Man Booker prize in 2015. In 2021 Jamaica was named the Leading Adventure Tourism Destination and the Leading Nature Destination in the Caribbean at the World Travel Awards. In 2019, Toni-Ann Singh won the Miss World contest and became the fourth Jamaican to do so.

While we have been known for our creative talents, Jamaica is now more and more being seen as a serious player in the world of business. In 2019 the Jamaica Stock Exchange gained recognition as the best-performing stock exchange in the world.

We can keep listing accomplishment after accomplishment by Jamaica and Jamaicans all day and given the chance we will gladly do so because as Jamaicans we love to highlight our country's achievements.

Asked to explain how a country so small is recognised for achieving so much we explain it with the one Jamaican phrase that says it all, "Wi likkle but wi tallawah".

'Likkle' means little. 'Tallawah' may be defined to you by Jamaicans as strong, strong-willed, powerful, resilient or tough.

It's a favourite line that we repeat whenever we hear of some new Jamaican accomplishment. We use it to explain an inherent quality of over-achievement.

I have thought a lot about this. But I also think about the challenges our country continues to face such as poverty, a need for greater infrastructure, the gap between where our industries are at the moment and where they need to be, our crime situation and improvements to social services, etc.

These challenges, to my mind, do not negate the idea of "likkle but tallawah". On the contrary, as a professional in the tourist industry which has seen advancement in leaps and bounds over the years, thanks to hard work and meticulous organization, I believe that the idea of "likkle but tallawah" can be used to transcend the challenges we face.

Imagine if we evolved the phrase "likkle but tallawah" from a description or explanation of our accomplishments to a way of life or lifestyle designed to take us from resilient to a state of thriving and self-realisation. Imagine if we took it from merely accomplishing great things in the face of adversity to actually overcoming, reducing, foreseeing and even eliminating adversity.

"Likkle but tallawah" so far has been proof of what we can do. Now, let us use it to do what we must do.

Is that too big to ask? I don't think so. And I believe Jamaicans have already begun to realize that we can utilise our greatest resource, our people, to take us to a higher level of existence, one where we all benefit from our 'tallawah' nature together as a nation.

Take for example the tourism sector for which I can speak. Jamaica has gained recognition for decades as a tourist destination and enjoys increasing numbers of visitors.

But, the industry in recent years has not sat back to merely enjoy its status. Instead, we have tried to accelerate our growth, expand and diversify the product and create new experiences. We recognised our inherent strength and decided to use it as a vehicle for growth.

We have created linkages to other industries to expose food, culture, events and products to visitors. We are creating immersive experiences to meet the needs of the global traveller.

We are working to stimulate small and medium-sized enterprises within the industry so more can benefit from its rewards.

This is what I mean by turning "tallawah" from a mere description to make it a way of life, an attitude, a job, a mission.

With Industry 5.0 technology evolution, "wi likkle but we tallawah" takes on a new landscape. Jamaicans can literally stay in their 'yard' and become a worldwide influencer, tech entrepreneur or distribution mastermind. With the 'tallawah' mindset driven to overcome adversity young Jamaicans can forge ahead in this new world with total confidence. It will not matter which 'likkle' district you come from, which 'likkle' basic school you went to or even how 'likkle' money you have. The opportunity to receive and utilise knowledge is closer at hand than ever before and the best of Jamaica is still yet to be revealed.

I am sure other professionals from various Jamaican industries can tell you of new initiatives and programmes to take our economy forward. What I am suggesting is not a new invention, but it is something we should do more of. If we see our greatness not just as our past and present accomplishments, but as a mission to accomplish more, to secure a brighter future and realise our full potential, we will thrive.

Our unique Jamaican jerk cuisine has gained fame all around the world. It is the first dish many visitors ask for when they come to the island. Yes, that plate of jerked chicken or jerk edpork is another example of "wi likkle but wi tallawah", but what I am saying is that the greatness of it isn't the food itself, it is in the recipe.

"Wi likkle but wi tallawah" can be the rallying call and 'our recipe' for a greater tomorrow.

Nicola Madden-Greig is President of the Caribbean Hotel and Tourism Association (CHTA).

THE MICO UNIVERSITY COLLEGE

The Mico University College has been the region's flagship teacher-training institution for over 185 years. This is no easy feat, considering the college's long history of challenges: structural damages due to repeat fires, earthquakes, the 1918 pandemic, two world wars and the two-time closure of its campus. Through it all, The Mico survived and outlived many institutions of its time. Amid the odds, the college has also anchored and supported Jamaica, particularly during its historical watershed eras, it was there at Emancipation, the Morant Bay Uprising, during the failed West Indies Federation and at Independence. Today, staff and graduates continue to make monumental contributions to education and leadership globally.

Self-Transforming

The Mico has self-transformed, as well, evolving from the Mico Institution to a university college with institutional accreditation. Nevertheless, the College remains grounded by its vision, mission and core values: leadership, excellence in performance, service to others, and integrity.

Remaining Relevant and Responsive

Mico has also progressed because of its forward-thinking approach to higher education. Note that in 2016, two years before the largest medical pandemic of modern history, we launched the Smart College Programme and began offering blended learning options for some courses. As a result, the staff was able to quickly pivot at the onset of the Coronavirus and deliver high-quality online instruction to more than 2000 students.

What's more is that The Mico continues to enhance and expand its programme offerings, in response to Jamaica's changing needs. For instance, through its School of Continuing Studies, in-service professionals and others can upskill by pursuing courses in robotics, STEM methodologies, geographic information systems, animation and more. The College is also partnering with the STEM for Life Foundation and the Ministry of Education to establish a national STEAM centre on campus. This development will fuel a more robust STEAM culture locally while promoting the government's agenda of more critical and creative thinking and engagements.

Remaining Inclusive

True to its core, The Mico has remained inclusive, over the years, and has unfailingly promoted tolerance, respect, and empathy for all. Visually impaired students have been accommodated and assisted through various undergraduate programmes, and many have graduated to teach, empower, and inspire their own charges. The college's inclusivity is also marked by its non-denominational status. In fact, each year, students from diverse religious backgrounds are welcomed and given equal opportunities to learn, innovate, and shine in a range of disciplines.

Supporting National Development

Further, The Mico has consistently served others. So, although the pandemic affected its coffers, the College has never relented at giving back. With the help of the Mico Old Students Association (MOSA), for example, several scholarships have been awarded to students. In addition to this, last December the College's Student Services Department led a Christmas wish list initiative that saw many undergraduates benefitting from bursaries, groceries, laptops and tablets.

The Pre-University Men's Programme (PUMP) is another testament of the College's unswerving devotion to national development. Thanks to this initiative, hundreds of males, the most vulnerable in our society, have become teacher certified and self-sufficient. Also, because of PUMP, more male educators are helming classrooms at all levels of Jamaica's school system.

Lecturers, too, have been very committed and benevolent throughout the years. They have voluntarily trained other teachers in instructional technology, literacy instruction, and STEAM integration. In-service teachers, including those at some of Jamaica's inner-city schools, have also been coached and mentored through Mico's outreach projects. Additionally, students have generously volunteered their time and talents for the collective good of the Jamaican citizenry. Some have tutored struggling readers, while others have assisted with homework and behaviour modification programmes at neighbouring schools.

Researching and Igniting Change

On top of these altruistic acts, The Mico has assisted in advancing local scholarship through its Institute of Technological and Educational Research (ITER), annual research day proceedings, and online conferences. Through webinars, peer-reviewed journals, local newspapers, and international online blogs, members of staff have also shared best practices for curriculum development, classroom instruction, and transformative leadership.

Producing Outstanding Graduates

The Mico prides itself in producing some of the most distinguished stalwarts in society: clergies, missionaries, entrepreneurs, governors-general and noble politicians who have championed and piloted local reforms. Graduates are also leading their institutions as principals, vice-principals, heads of departments, and supervisors. Several have been recruited to teach in the United Kingdom, the Middle East, Asia, and elsewhere. Some have been named teachers of the year in the United States, and many others are spearheading community-building projects islandwide.

Still, The Mico, more than ever, is committed to its mantra and core values. Staff and students are resolute in their mission to make Jamaica "the place of choice to live, work, raise families and do business" (Vision 2030).

President of The Mico University College, Dr. Asburn Pinnock.

"Carreras Limited is 60 years this year and we are pleased to have journeyed with our island home Jamaica since the very beginning.

We remain inspired by our ardent and diligent management and staff as well as the many valued customers and stakeholders we have had over the years.

We are extremely thankful to our consumers for making us a household name and including our products in their adult basket of goods. Thank you for your never-ending loyalty and trust in the Carreras brand.

As we look towards the future, let us boldly recommit ourselves to providing even greater service to our country while delivering "A Better Tomorrow" for all!"

Raoul Glynn,
Managing Director

Happy 60th anniversary team Carreras!
&
Happy 60 years of independence Jamaica!

Dwayne, Ashelle, Donovan, Nakisha, Olivia, Cloyd, Craig, Jodian, Kimesha, Rhoja, Gregory, Andre, Dane, Nicole, Marvin, Shaniel, Phallon, Jodi-Ann, Howard, Kadian, Shaneele, Sasha, Anthony, Jamell, Clayon, Khafre, Raoul, Sashelle, Efrey, Shane, Marvia, Orlando, Corretta, Rudgell, Daron, Kemmo, Rohan, Camille, Kacey-Ann, Raschida, Andrew, Mary, Sandrea, Jermaine, Rochelle, Chevelle, Gharri, Thalia, Romain, Chantell, Sowian, Alibaster, Kevin, Noel, Desmond, Jermaine, Daidrey, Kevin, Michaldo, Nadine, Darrien, Edward, Richard, Ebonique, Byron, Andre, Temoy, Nyjoma, Ishmael, Aeisha, Daniel, Shane, Jason, Rickard, Donald, Clive, Samantha, Lloyd, Alicia, Kurt, Danuta, Bettiann, Kedisha, Wesley, Asheaka, Dwayne, Hakeem, Dextrose, Sean-Roy, Chrisam, Dwaine, Tasheann, Verona, Orlando, Omara

SOAP BOX
The parties speak in a new feature starting today with columns from the PNP on property taxes and the JLP on the ToJ.
Page 6A

The Sunday Gleaner

VOLUME XLVIII, NO. 47 KINGSTON, JAMAICA November 28, 1993 92 PAGES US2.50

Sunday Index
Perspective....6A
Parish....7
Opinions....8A
Commentaries....9A
Want Ads....11-15A
Auto Feature....19-24A
Court....25A
Death Notices....30,31A
Sports....1-3B
Entertainment....1C,D
Business....1E

Lisa is Miss World

Third Jamaican to win title

TOP OF THE WORLD — Jamaica's lovely Lisa Hanna rode off with the title of Miss World 1993 yesterday, and prizes totalling US$185,000, including an Alfa Romeo motorcar.

MISS JAMAICA, 18-year-old Lisa Hanna, yesterday topped a field of 80 competitors from across the globe to win the Miss World 1993 title in a singing and dancing extravaganza which impressed the judges in South Africa and set off national rejoicing here.

Lisa charmed the crowd and judges at the South African resort of Sun City with her exuberant personality to win the title previously held by Julia Kurotchinka of Russia.

The 5 foot 7 inch brown-eyed beauty from St. Andrew became the third Jamaican to wear the coveted crown, the first since Cindy Breakespeare took the title in 1976, 17 years ago. Carol Crawford also won in 1963.

Jacqueline Mofokeng, 21, who was the first black woman to win the Miss South Africa title, was first runner-up. Miss Philippines, 19-year-old Sharmaine Gutierrez, was second runner-up.

Lisa's win, which carries prizes worth US$185,000, including an Alfa Romeo motorcar, was watched by an estimated 1.2 billion broadcast audience around the world.Jamaicans were also glued to their television sets to witness the announcement, made at about 2 p.m., which set off scenes of celebration as congratulatory messages poured into local media houses from all sections of society.

In a statement issued yesterday Prime Minister P. J. Patterson said:

"On behalf of the Government and people of Jamaica and on my own behalf, I extend to you my warmest congratulations on winning the Miss World crown. You have proved once again that Jamaicans are among the best in the world in every field of endeavour."

A statement to Lisa from the Jamaica Labour Party leader Edward Seaga said: "All Jamaica is proud and joins in celebrating with you on your victorious and deserving achievement of the Miss World Beauty Pagaent crown. With beauty, intelligence and talent you have put Jamaica on top of the world."

Lisa's father, Rene, who watched the contest on television was ecstatic over the achievements of his youngest child.

Pride

"I feel proud for the people of Jamaica," he said. "I also feel proud of the people who helped to make the decision to give her the title. I personally know she is deserving of the title. I am looking forward to her coming home."

Lisa's mother Shirley accompanied her to the contest in South Africa.

Former, beauty queens also joined in the celebrations and offered congratulations. Cindy Breakspeare Tavares-Finson said: "I am over the moon and very happy for her. I am sure she will do a great job for Jamaica."

Barry Wilson, Lisa's personal fitness trainer at the Spartan Health Club, told **The Sunday Gleaner** that he was very excited, ecstatic and happy.

"She deserves it," he said. "Look at how she answered her questions. Her body was well conditioned."

Kingsley Cooper, executive chairman of the Pulse investments, the modeling agency which released Lisa from her contract for a year so she could participate in both the Miss Jamaica and Miss World contests, also expressed delight.

"We are definitely thrilled and overjoyed by Lisa's success," he said.

Entertainer Juliet Prowse, actor Lou Gossett Jr., novelist Frederick Forsyth, martial arts actor Jackie Chan, model and actress Twiggy, actress and singer Grace Jones and model Christie Brinkley chose Miss Hanna from among 80 contestants.

This story was compiled from local and overseas wire reports.

Spotlight on some of our other queens

JAMAICA has enjoyed tremendous success in the Miss World competition. The following is a listing of some of the achievements:

- 1963 Carol Crawford crowned Miss World. The Government issued a postage stamp in her honour.
- 1973 — Patsy Yuen placed third, but actually served as Miss World, when the winner Miss USA was disgraced.
- 1976 — Cindy Breakspeare crowned Miss World.
- 1981 — Sandra Cunningham placed third.
- 1983 — Cathy Levy placed fourth.
- 1991 — Sandra Foster placed fourth in Miss World. There were two sections to that contest. Judges in the South African part of the contest placed her second.
- 1993 — Lisa Hanna crowned Miss World.

All Jamaica salutes Lisa Hanna

THOUSANDS of Jamaicans were elated when Jamaica's Lisa Hanna was crowned the 1993 Miss World yesterday afternoon. Many screamed their heads off and sprung in the air in jubilation. The Sunday Gleaner spoke with several women who related their feelings on the achievement.

Dorrette Brown (police) —"I was full of emotion, being that it was somebody I knew personally. Lisa was always humble and full of confidence. She was somebody who always stood out in my mind because of her qualities."

E. Plummer (branch manager — Homelectrix) — "I got goose pimples and was overjoyed. I could not help leaping in the air and screaming.

Lorraine Long (self employed) — "I screammed when she won. I am happy for her and was always confident that she would have won. It is full time a black woman take the crown."

Renae Williams (hairdresser) — "I feel great and happy for her. When she was announed as the winner, I jumped in the air and screamed."

Joan Senior (hairdresser) — "I feel real good to know that a Jamaican woman can represent us ... and make us look big.

Althea McPherson (self employed) — "I wish her all the best in life and hope she keeps up the good work. I am proud of her."

Hopie Gibbs — "I feel good for her, after such a long time a Jamaican finally came out on top and make our country real proud."

Hiliary Lawrence — "I am too happy. It is a long time. I am proud of her because she make Jamaica proud. They can't stop us now."

Lisa charmed the crowd and judges at the South African resort of Sun City with her exuberant personality to win...

1993

The Gleaner

ESTABLISHED 1834

VOLUME 164 NO. 126 KINGSTON, JAMAICA, FRIDAY, MAY 29, 1998 44 PAGES $12

OFF SHORE
FOR THE NAMES YOU KNOW
Anmor's (Obviously).
70B King Street/The Village Mall

Spelling Bee triumph!

-Reuters

WASHINGTON - Jody-Anne Maxwell, a 12-year-old from Kingston, Jamaica, hoists her trophy with the aide of Rich Boehne, vice-president of corporate communications for E.W. Scripps, after she won the 71st annual Scripps Howard National Spelling Bee, yesterday in Washington D.C. ■

❑ Jody-Anne Maxwell, 12, wins US championship

JAMAICA'S 1997 national Gleaner/Children's Own Spelling Bee champion, 12-year-old Jody-Anne Maxwell, emerged victorious yesterday in the Scripps Howard National Spelling Bee competition in Washington, D.C., becoming the first person outside of the USA to win the coveted championship.

She was one of three Jamaican contestants, including Westwood High School's Bettina McLean, and Montego Bay High's Haydee Lindo. This was the second year that Jamaica was entering the Scripps Howard competition.

A straight A student of Ardenne High School in St. Andrew, Jody-Anne won last year in the 38th All-Island Gleaner\Children's Own Spelling Bee Competition while she was a student at Ardenne Preparatory and the St. Andrew Parish Champion.

In that competition, Bettina, the St. Ann champion representing Ocho Rios Primary, placed second, while third place went to Haydee, then a student of Mt. Alvernia Preparatory, who was the St. James parish champion.

Another contestant in the Scripps Howard Spelling Bee, representing the Bahamas, was born in Jamaica of Jamaican parents, **The Gleaner** was told.

Bettina made it to the seventh of the 11 rounds this year, finishing in the top 10.

According to a Reuters report, Jody-Anne clinched the title in the 71-year-old competition with the word "chiaroscurist," an artist who works with the arrangement of light and dark parts in a pictorial work.

The champion said the hardest moment came in the first round of the finals, when she had to spell the word "alveolate", which means pitted like a honeycomb.

"That was the ice breaker," she told reporters after her victory. "I was really nervous before I spelled that."

Maxwell beat out Prem Murthy Trivedi of Neptune, N.J., who was competing in his fourth national finals. Trivedi finished as runner-up for the second year in a row, faltering on "prairillon," meaning small meadow or tract of grassland.

Maxwell survived the two-day finals competition by carefully breaking down each word, often asking for a word's pronunciation many times and spending minutes in thought with her head down before slowly spelling the word.

Along the way to victory, Maxwell, a seventh grader at Ardenne High School in

CONTINUES ON A3

INSIDE
COMMENT A4
When people rebel – John Rapley
FEATURE B8
Showtime
Entertainers' charity – not an ego thing
Financial Gleaner
The oils heat up
CARTOONS C12
CLASSIFIED B9
MEMORIAM B11
SPORT B1

PM wants unified strategy to fight drug traffickers

DESCRIBING DRUG traffickers as "peddlers of death" and "the world's most dreaded menace," Prime Minister P.J. Patterson said yesterday his administration would not tire in its battle to eradicate narcotics.

While acknowledging that the drug cartels had vast resources at their disposal, Mr. Patterson called for a hemispheric strategy backed by adequate finances to defeat drug trafficking.

Speaking before a gathering of the military heads of 15 nations and observers from several other countries in New Kingston, the Prime Minister called for a unified response to defeat what a United Nations report identified as the single largest industry in the world.

The drug cartels, the Prime Minister said, were "highly-organised, hardly any longer clandestine, technologically sophisticated, rotten rich, and unlike our security forces have access to all and any resource they need to carry out their nefarious activity."

The Prime Minister was the guest speaker at the opening ceremony of the 14th Caribbean Island Nations Security Conference (CINSEC) at Le Meridien Jamaica Pegasus Hotel.

Mr. Patterson said drug dons had access to unlimited financial resources, modern computer software and some of the best professional brains.

P.J. Patterson ■

"What is more, these individuals and organisations have diversified their activities into such areas as arms trafficking, money laundering, terrorism and the illegal movement of people," he said.

Mr. Patterson said drug traffickers had infiltrated "the legal economic, administrative and in some cases the political arms of some of the countries in which they operate.

"In the same way that the criminal elements engaged in wide-scale narco trafficking and other illegal activities, have found strength in banding together, so too must we combine our resources of money, intelligence, skill and business and security acumen, to wage a concerted war against the forces of evil which threaten our very survival," he said.

In a comment seemingly aimed at the United States, Mr. Patterson called on the authorities to prevent illegal firearms coming into other countries. "And in the same way that we in the Caribbean are expected to take every effort to sanitise our exports into other areas, we expect other countries to make every effort to sanitise their exports into our areas including a prevention of illegal weapons," he said.

The conference, which ends today, is focusing mainly on counter-drug operations but will look at disaster preparedness and response.

1998

Reggae Boyz Qualify for France World Cup

The Gleaner

Established 1834

VOLUME 164 NO. 131 KINGSTON, JAMAICA, THURSDAY, JUNE 4, 1998 32 PAGES $13

France, here we come!

– Junior Dowie

Members of Jamaica's national football team with Prime Minister P.J. Patterson at Jamaica House yesterday morning, just before departing for the World Cup finals in France. Also in picture are Professor René Simoes, technical director of the team, and Captain Horace Burrell, president of the Jamaica Football Federation (JFF). ■

❑ *Reggae Boyz off to World Cup finals*

PRIME MINISTER P.J. Patterson yesterday urged members of the national football team, to "go with God, dignity and pride" as they participate in the World Cup finals.

The Prime Minister spoke at a send-off function attended by the players and the football management at Jamaica House prior to their departure for France.

"The televisions will be on you, the journalists will be at you. You must behave yourselves and know what you do or say," he cautioned.

"This is a historic moment for all Jamaicans, whether they live at home or abroad," Mr. Patterson said, "but remember the whole world will be watching us. You should endeavour to conduct yourselves in a manner that will be to your credit as well as that of the country and your individual clubs."

The Prime Minister, who had promised during the World Cup build-up that "I will see you in France", will be leading a Government delegation to the event early next week.

Mr. Patterson presented the national team and its coaching staff with replicas of the Jamaican Coat of Arms for their lapels.

See related story on Page B1.

March 1998 – The Reggae Boys and Technical Director, Rene Simoes strike a camaraderie pose with Lola Chin Sang (far left) and Courts Director Hayden Singh, (fifth from left) at the sponsorship Ceremony held at Le Meridien. This was the highlight of all sponsors coming together to plan and support the Jamaica team on their last lap to France.

Technical Director, Renee Simoes is hoisted after Jamaica drew with Mexico in their CONCACAF final round qualifier at the National Stadium in 1997, which marked Jamaica's qualification for the 1998 World Cup Finals in France. Looking on are Reggae Boyz Deon Burton (right) and Aaron Lawrence (centre).

1998

'Wi Likkle But Wi Tallawah': An Indomitable Spirit to Honour at Jamaica 60

Joey Issa

As the country looks forward to its 60th anniversary of Independence, a great gift for the nation would be the official recognition and celebration of what's best about Jamaica, which undoubtedly, is the image its people have of themselves, 'Wi likkle but wi tallawah' carries with it much bragging rights around the globe.

This well-known phrase reportedly has its genesis in a celebrated Hope Zoo tiger cub named *Tallawah* which fell very sick, but refused to die, and when it eventually passed way beyond its limit of endurance, in 1966, it took two Bengal tigers from the US to replace Tallawah, according to a 1968 article in the *Daily Gleaner.*

It is this indomitable spirit that best defines who we are as Jamaicans, strong, resilient and not to be underestimated. That spirit has not waned, from our struggles for freedom from enslavement and colonial rule and oppression to today's achievements against all odds.

The 'Tallawah' spirit has stood the test of time as "it is in our veins", to quote former Prime Minister Portia Simpson Miller. It is an endemic Jamaican quality that resonates with the biblical story of David taking on Goliath and Bob Marley's iconic 1973 hit song, *Small Axe*: "If you are a big tree, we are the small axe."

Although citizens throughout the world can lay claim to an indomitable similar fighting spirit, the Jamaican quality is like no other in the way it is revered at home and feared around the globe, and for good reason. A good example is the well-known posture of Olympic 100-metre champion and world record-holder over the distance, Usain Bolt. This posture which he takes before taking his mark, is said to have intimidated and weakened opponents throughout his career. Similarly, hurdler Megan Tapper who was told she was too short in stature to leap over the hurdles to succeed in the event, became a bronze medallist in the 100 metres at the 2020 Tokyo Olympics, and afterwards demonstrated that indomitable Jamaican spirit with the now famous dance move that has captured the imagination of the international media and young people all over the world.

The Jamaican attitude is a source of pride for every citizen. It is easily identified in every major feat achieved by the country as it lies within every Jamaican whether rich or poor, young or old, here or abroad.

'Likkle but tallawah' is the single most important trait that drives, inspires and empowers Jamaicans to achieve. It is the determination to succeed that brings out the necessary hard work which every successful child, man and woman in every sphere of life has had to put in.

The Jamaican spirit is an all-inclusive concept as it is associated with feats in every aspect of Jamaican life, from the cart vendor who aspires to have his own shop, to the poor parent who wants the child to become a doctor, lawyer or successful professional.

Dare to dream is a characteristic of the Jamaican indomitable spirit and can be found on every street corner and in communities across the country.

Unlike other good things about Jamaica, whether it's our food, beaches, or luminaries, all of which have a limited shelf life and do not automatically transcend from one generation to the next, the indomitable Jamaican spirit is forever present. It is embedded in our genetic code. Why else would Jamaica outstrip so many countries in significant achievements per capita, including the mighty US, which is about 900 times larger and the UK, 22 times larger than Jamaica?

Jamaica's emboldened attitude has also been manifested in our foreign policy positions over several administrations since Independence. For it is this audacious character and spirit that reportedly led Jamaica to become the first country to put a trade embargo on apartheid South Africa, even before we were an Independent nation. At the United Nations, it was Jamaica's initiative that led the world body to devote the year 1968 to human rights, a proposal which we first made in 1963. After Independence we became more emboldened, proposing to the United Nations in 1963 to devote a year to human rights, which it did, albeit five years later.

A year later in 1969 Jamaica is said to have done something that no other country had done before, that is, becoming a member of the Organisation of American States (OAS) while maintaining diplomatic relations with Cuba and refusing to put place sanctions or a trade embargo against on its close neighbour. (That same year the country also joined the Non-Aligned Movement – the new international economic order – and established closer relations with a number of African countries, and supported antiapartheid initiatives, including Cuban troops in southern Africa.

More recently, we were bold enough to criticised the US invasion of Iraq and allowed exiled former president of Haiti safe stay on the island.

As with foreign policy, Jamaica's attitude of choice is reflected most notably in our achievements in sport and music, which since Independence continue to contribute to the economy and nation-building, especially the youths, giving Jamaica a fighting chance to navigate the post-Independence era. And who best represents that strong, fearless and strong-willed Jamaican spirit than Bob Marley, who brought two fierce political rivals together at a pivotal moment in Jamaica's political history, and Usain Bolt who captured the imagination of the world with his never-before-seen lightning speed?

Thus, if a referendum were to be held to pay homage to that indomitable Jamaican spirit that inspires and enthuses devotion to success, and Marley and Bolt are on the list for National Hero status my vote would be yes, yes, yes!

Joey Issa is the founder of the Cool Group of Companies.

*Editorial note: Like so many of Marley's lyrics, this one is not original, but comes from an African proverb.

Tribute to Trelawny Yellow Yam

M.A. Stewart-Hinchcliffe

The parish of Trelawny is in the county of Cornwall in northwest Jamaica. Its capital is Falmouth. It is bordered by the parishes of St. Ann in the east, St. James in the west, and St. Elizabeth and Manchester in the south.

Trelawny is the parish of my birth, specifically the district of Lorrimers, which borders on the district of Battersea, which is in the neighbouring parish of St. Ann.

What makes reference to this location area of particular interest is its reputation as Jamaica's 'yam belt,' with the dominant yam being the Trelawny yellow yam.

Trelawny is also famous for its athletes, the standout being Usain St. Leo Bolt, but that is for a different time and place. I too had my days as an athlete at Excelsior High School in Kingston where I was hard to beat on the track, while also playing softball, and the centre-forward position on the hockey team. My pursuits way back then could have been attributed to my then-diet of yellow yam. Usain Bolt's father is also said to be of the view that his son's athletics prowess is due to his diet of yellow yam. There were studies done on this premise, of which I was included as part of the sample with academics and other athletes, but the effect of a yellow yam diet has remained unproven.

Salute Trelawny Yellow Yam Farmer

What is indisputable though is yellow yam as an agricultural product holds pride of place for investment as there is ready market – high demand on the local and export markets, and marketing and production information

1. *Yellow yams on the way to be prepared for export, Lorrimers, Trelawny*
2. *Yam field in early growth*

have been readily available throughthe Rural Agricultural Development Agency (RADA) of the Ministry of Agriculture and Fisheries. Trelawny yellow yam has developed into diversified uses, but mostly consumed in its cooked form, whether as the base food dish, in soups, fried chips, yam rundung, stews and salads. Wherever a starch-based diet is, Trelawny yellow yam is ever present.

The versality of yellow yam has also earned its place among vegetables – roasted, fried, boiled and baked.

Yam Varieties

While there are over 18 different varieties of yam grown across Jamaica, the most popular is yellow yam. Other yams include Sweet and Negro, Renta, St. Vincent, Yampie and Tau Yam. Yams are exported to the UK, USA and Canada. Yellow yam far exceeds others, such as Negro and Sweet yams.

A Yellow Yam Growing Field Takes Its Place

As we celebrate the 'best of Jamaica 60' marking our Independence Jubilee, 2022, we must be mindful of the areas in the economy, our culture, our arts, our climate, our people, our music, our business that come together to make Jamaica great. Here in south Trelawny, the yellow yam, from planting, to growing, and reaping; from farm to table; to export markets and to sustaining the livelihood of the farming community, such as Lorrimers, Low River along the corridor from north Manchester through south Trelawny in the heart of the Cockpit Country, stands ready as an avenue for investment.

3

4

3. *Jermain Williams, yam farmer with freshly reaped yellow yams at Lorrimers, Trelawny.*
4. *A mature yam field ready for reaping.*

(Photos contributed by Douglas and Christopher Stewart)

Yam Festival

Trelawny yellow yam is a marker for 60 years of Jamaica's Independence with the emergence of Trelawny Yam Festival, which started out as a major tourist attraction on Easter Monday, 1997 organized by the Southern Trelawny Environmental Agency. The purpose was a fundraiser to support the local community and to celebrate yam as an important food item and the culture of Trelawny. The festival, though short lived, showcased the versatility of yam from production and products, including yam cake, bun, wine, flour, pudding, and punch. As with any festival there were demonstrations and competitions for community members and schools.

(Jamaica's Yellow Yam Festival a Major Tourist Attraction on Easter Monday; by Bridget Boalie, April 22, 2019).

Trelawny yellow yam Salutes the 'Best of Jamaica 60' in the year of Jamaica Independence Jubilee, 2022.

5. Freshly reaped yellow yam at Lorrimers, Trelawny.

6. Cyrus Rowe showing off the best of his crop at Lorrimers, Trelawny.

Audrey Hinchcliffe is Chairman and CEO of Manpower & Maintenance Services Limited.

The People:

THE SPIRIT AND CONTINUED SHOW OF RESILIENCE OF THE PEOPLE OF JAMAICA

Chris Williams

"Being the change; creating the change in our country."

When we think about 'the best of Jamaica', a pause occurs with the realisation that Jamaica would not be what it is without the people behind it.

Despite being a small island with a population of approximately 2.9 million, this 'likkle' island has positioned itself on the grid internationally as a force, thanks to the people, bringing to life the expression, '*we likkle but we tallawah*'.

Our people, 'out of many', add flavour and spice in a unique way with a melting pot that lends to a rich culture and strong history, well known for sports like track and field, entertainment, especially music, food, the beauty of the country, and overall, our persona.

It is about all that we are and who we are. It is about being Jamaican, which many might forget the privilege, pride and joy that it brings.

We have the fastest man, the fastest woman, the best parties, the best beaches, incredible entrepreneurial spirit and a 'vibe' unlike any other – laced with reggae and synonymous with Bob Marley. As we reflect, the commonalities throughout the years which characterise the 'best of the best' are the drive and spirit that keep us going, our resilience, strength and tough attitude in our approach to life.

The people make up the country and build up the country, who contribute, create, and work hard to make it what it has been, what it is now and what it will be. We cannot look to commemorate anything of its 'Jamaicanness' without first recognizing who allowed for that thing to come into fruition in the first place.

We need to continue on the quest to develop the country by developing ourselves and building one another. 'No man is an island'; it takes a village.

There is so much to celebrate about Jamaica, but it all lies within the hands, hearts and minds of the people; each of us with vision, bright hopes, goals and dreams for our little country doing our part and acting in the best interest of our nation. We are fighters, winners, game-changers, trailblazers, movers and shakers. *We are likkle but tallawah.* What and who we are has been embedded within us and everything we do. Something I stand by is being the change you want to see. We are relentless in shaping our lives and our country and creating that change, at any cost. Hence, there is no doubt that the best is still yet to come, because we keep getting better and better.

Chris Williams is the Chief Executive Officer of Proven.

It All Starts
With an Idea.
For over 90 years, we've been helping Jamaicans make their ideas real. So count on us as you explore what's next for your home, business, farm and garden.
HL
Rapid
True Value
Agro
Hardware & Lumber Wholesale
Regency Blinds
www.hardwareandlumber.com

SUPREME VENTURES: INTERWOVEN INTO THE VERY FABRIC OF JAMAICA

The dawn of an Independent Jamaica in 1962 sparked the commercial and entrepreneurial journey of numerous home-grown visionaries. Supreme Ventures Limited (SVL) is one of those companies, forged by the vision of creating a strong and successful Jamaican brand.

As we pause to celebrate the country's 60th year of Independence, we also reflect on how the SVL brand has become interwoven into the very fabric of Jamaica.

Since our 2001 inception, SVL has become a household name and an indelible part of Jamaica's cultural landscape, synonymous with integrity, entertainment and winning. Our longevity and level of operational excellence has made us the standard-bearer for gaming nationally and in the wider region.

The place we currently hold in the hearts and minds of our customers and those we have touched outside of gaming has been hard won. It was built through continuous customer focus, clear-growth strategies, strong leadership, and a genuine drive for innovation.

Perhaps imbued with the indomitable Jamaican spirit, Supreme Ventures continues to break the mould and create new standards in the local business landscape. We have revolutionised gaming and commerce with thousands of Jamaicans having a stake in our operations as retailers or shareholders.

There are very few companies that can boast of a strong relationship with small businesses and micro-entrepreneurs in which both enterprises emerge as winners. Since 2001, our retailers, irrespective of the size and stature of their outlets, have been on the frontline of SVL operations. It is through their stores, shops, pharmacies, supermarkets, and store fronts, located in every nook and cranny of the island, that we conduct in excess of 97 million transactions per year.

Supreme Ventures has been a publicly listed company since 2006, giving every Jamaican the opportunity to own a share in the dream we are building towards every day.

We are committed to taking the bold steps needed to create a company that epitomises Jamaican business excellence. Not only have we expanded by building out our gaming enterprise through acquisitions and product development, such as the Supreme Scratchaz instant win scratch card launched in 2022, but we have also diversified our operational portfolio by venturing into new territories in Guyana and South Africa, into new markets, such as micro-lending through Supreme Ventures FinTech Limited, business services through the Supreme Ventures Business Hub, and we have begun the integration of digital into our operations. All our games can now be accessed via our suite of digital assets: SV Games, JustBet Mobile and MBet for horse racing at Caymanas Park and through simulcast. This is just the beginning of our continuous movement forward.

This is how Supreme Ventures was built and continues to thrive, on the dreams of the most resilient, tenacious, and determined people. We continue to build out this vision, making strong strategic decisions that expand our reach and depth of operation actively contributing to the strengthening of the Jamaican economy.

Supreme's impact has been tremendous. While our games are played largely for entertainment purposes, it cannot be denied that our winnings have fueled the dreams of gamers from all walks of life.

We are an undeniable force for the good of the Jamaican economy, circulating billions in revenues, fees, and prize payments annually. In 2021 we made the biggest contribution to government coffers – paying over $7.9 billion in government taxes and contributions supporting culture, health, arts, sports, and education.

The empathetic heart of our people beats strongly across the organisation, and we always remember that to whom much is given, much is also expected, and we have contributed billions to good causes focused on culture, health, arts, sports and education.

We are cognizant that our success is meaningless without ensuring that we support the most vulnerable in our society and this knowledge drives us to invest in building the infrastructure that protects them. We average a contribution of $2 billion every year to the government to be able to meet these needs, and in addition we also contribute through our own Supreme Ventures Foundation, the philanthropic arm of the SVL group.

In 2021, the Supreme Ventures Foundation continued its mission to improve this infrastructure through strategically designed programmes that positively impacted the lives of children in state care, retooled community enterprises and strengthened Jamaica's medical infrastructure to do our part in the fight against the COVID-19 pandemic that threatened Jamaica's social and economic stability.

We have done so much and there is so much left to do, but we are up to the task. We pledge to serve our island with humble pride and to play our part in making Jamaica the greatest nation in the region and indeed the world.

Supreme Ventures salutes Jamaica, the Land of Our Birth, Our Home on its Diamond Jubilee. We will forever be grateful to this wonderful nation for being the fertile soil of our growth and the rock upon which we have built a legacy that will remain unmatched and unwavering for years to come.

Cheers to 60!

SUPREME
VENTURES
FOUNDATION
1

20TH
ANNIVERSARY
Making Winners Everyday!
LOTTO
2

$259,000,000
A. RENNALDS
OCTOBER 1, 2021
SUPREME
VENTURES
A TICKET TO YOUR DREAMS!
LOTTO
3

An elated Jenny 'Miss Jenny' Brown riumphantly raises her trophy after being leclared the inaugural winner of the 2021 Supreme Heroes programme. SVF directors, Heather Goldson and Peter McConnell share in the moment. The Supreme Heroes programme was specifically designed o recognise and retool small and micro businesses that understand the importance of philanthropy and community development and extend themselves to exemplify what it neans every day.

Foundational team members, Assistant Manager Applications Candice Ewers, SVREL GM Lorna Gooden and Payroll Manager Mark Findley slice into the SVL 20th anniversary cake with Executive Chairman Gary Peart at the company's official celebratory breakfast held to recognise he milestone in 2021.

Without the dreams and aspirations of our players, Supreme Ventures Limited would not have achieved the amazing successes of he past 21 years. We have provided exciting games of chance to persons from all walks of life both inside and outside of Jamaica. Pictured is the first gamer to strike gold and nake history by playing on the SV Games App.

Celebrating 18 years! SVL executive chairman s all smiles at SVL's 18th anniversary celebration event with L-R Journalist Cliff Hughes, Prime Minister Andrew Holness, hen State Minister in the Ministry of ndustry, Commerce, Agriculture & Fisheries Floyd Green and then Minister of Industry, Commerce, Agriculture and Fisheries Audley Shaw.

Prime Sports CEO Xesus Johnston and Executive Chairman Gary Peart sharing n the winning moment of Olympian and national champion Shelly-Ann Fraser-Pryce after she claimed the sprint double at the 2021 Supreme Ventures National Senior Athletics Championship. The company has been a big supporter of sports in Jamaica, investing nillions to develop the next generation of world-beaters.

Executive Chairman Gary Peart (centre) nakes the official handover of a mobile ultrasound machine to the University Hospital of the West Indies diagnostic department from the Supreme Ventures Foundation. This over $20 million nvestment in the health of Jamaicans in the wake of the 2020 COVID-19 pandemic also allowed the institution to progress its journey nto the digitization of their management operating system.

Emancipation Park Opens in Blaze of Lights and Music

The much, anticipated Emancipation Park in New Kingston opened last night in a blaze of lights, music and some patriotic, but fiery speeches on the subject of Emancipation.

The full beauty of the venue was brought into focus just before 9 p.m. when the lights and fountains were turned on. This was preceded by the planting of two trees, one each by Prime Minister P.J. Patterson and Governor-General Sir Howard Cooke, to mark the occasion.

Jamaica Labour Party spokesman on housing and the environment, Andrew Holness, represented Opposition Leader Edward Seaga, who left the island earlier yesterday.

In a fiery speech, often punctuated by loud applause, president of the Private Sector Organization of Jamaica and Gleaner chairman, Oliver Clarke, suggested that a great disservice would be done to Jamaica, if in commemorating Emancipation, the focus was only on 1838 (the year of Emancipation from slavery).

– Published August 1, 2002

Governor-General, Sir Howard Cooke (second right), gets some help in planting a tree symbolising the opening of Emancipation Park, New Kingston, on Wednesday, July 31, 2002. Looking on at second left is Prime Minister P.J. Patterson, who also planted a tree.

2002

2002

The Gleaner

ESTABLISHED 1834

THE GLEANER | www.jamaica-gleaner.com VOLUME 168 NO. 43 KINGSTON, JAMAICA 28 PAGES TUESDAY, FEBRUARY 19, 2002 $15

CARIBBEAN

Panday blamed

Team Unity political leader blames former PM Basdeo Panday for rise in crime in Trinidad & Tobago. **A8**

SPORT

On top

Williams bags five wickets as Jamaica whips Leeward Islands...**B1**

ENTERTAINMENT

Evening of Love

Love songs galore from Bryson and Flack...**C1**

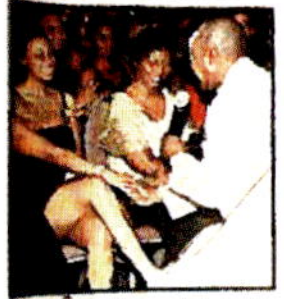

INDEX

NEWS	A2
EDITORIAL	A4
LETTERS	A5
AMERICAS	A6
INTERNATIONAL	A7
CARIBBEAN	A8
FINANCIAL	A10
SPORT	B1
ENTERTAINMENT	C1
MOVIES	C1
TV GUIDE	C2
PUZZLES	C3
HOROSCOPE	C4
CLASSIFIED	C5
MEMORIAM	C8

KIN. Windy 30ºC

MOBAY Windy 28ºC

MAND. P. Cloudy 27ºC

MURDER UPDATE

Police reports indicate that 124 persons, including a policeman, have died violently in Jamaica since January 1.

Royal welcome

RUDOLPH BROWN PHOTOS/Staff Photographer

Her Majesty, Queen Elizabeth II accompanied by His Royal Highness, Prince Philip arrived in the island yesterday. The couple is in Jamaica on a three-day visit, the first overseas trip of the Golden Jubilee to mark the Queen's 50th year as head of the British Monarchy and dependent territories.

■ See pictorial Page A2.

Queen Elizabeth II arrives

Rastas demand repatriation help

Leonardo Blair and Patricia Watson
Staff Reporters

CLAD IN a soft peach-coloured suit and matching hat, Queen Elizabeth II, arrived at the Norman Manley Airport yesterday on her sixth visit to the island as a 21-gun salute boomed from the cannon reserved for heads of states.

In this her Jubilee year, the 75-year-old monarch is on the first leg of 15 days of travel that will see her visiting Jamaica, Canada, New Zealand and Australia, all former colonies of Britain. The Queen's last visit to Jamaica was in 1994.

As she made her way down the steps from the aircraft, the Queen, accompanied by The Duke of Edinburgh, Prince Philip, was greeted by Governor-General Sir Howard Cooke and Lady Cooke, then Prime Minister P.J Patterson.

After the Jamaican National Anthem was played, the Queen, escorted by Major General John Simmonds inspected the 100 member-strong Jamaica Defence Force honour guard dressed in their scarlet uniforms, while the Jamaica Constabulary Force band played a medley of tunes.

She was later introduced to scores of public officials including Opposition Leader Edward

Please see **WELCOME, A3**

Qeen Elizabeth II (second right) greets Carla Seaga (left) wife of the Leader of the Opposition, Edward Seaga (second left) on her arrival in Jamaica yesterday. Looking on is Prime Minister P.J. Patterson (right) and Information Minister Colin Campbell (centre).

PNP scandals send over $6b down the drain

Vernon Daley
Staff Reporter

THE EMERGING controversy surrounding the National Housing Development Corporation (NHDC) is the latest in at least six major money scandals to hit the governing People's National Party since it took office 13 years ago.

Combined, these scandals have resulted in billions of tax dollars going down the drain.

However, the party is not overly perturbed by public rumblings over allegations of mismanagement and corruption in the Government and remains convinced that its bid for a fourth consecutive term in office remains viable.

"In terms of the electorate, the average person does not even know about these things," said party general-secretary, Maxine Henry-Wilson. She referred to a recent opinion poll which revealed that most Jamaicans were not aware of the NetServ scandal which broke late last year.

She said the party has not been affected on the ground by allegations of corruption and ineptitude because persons were aware that much of the public controversy was without substance and was linked to politicking.

The latest scandal to rock the Government involves NHDC and the Operation Pride housing projects that it administers. There are allegations of corruption and mismanagement at the NHDC, where there was a $35 million overpayment on a Operation Pride housing project.

Jamaica Labour Party spokesman on Finance, Audley Shaw, brought the issue to the fore last week while addressing a function on corruption. It also emerged that a study commissioned by the NHDC on 10 of the 100 Operation Pride projects, revealed that they are likely to overrun their original cost by $5.5 billion.

Prime Minister P.J. Patterson has since announced a four-man commission to review the

Please see **SCANDAL, A3**

PNP GOV'T MONEY SCANDALS

Shell Waiver (1991)	$29.5 million
Zinc (1989)	$500 million
Furniture (1991)	$10.6 million
Public Sector	
Salary (1998	$60 million
NetServ (2001)	$220 million
Operation Pride/NHDC	
(1997-present)	$5.5 billion projected
TOTAL	**$6.320 billion**

Her Majesty, Queen Elizabeth II accompanied by His Royal Highness, Prince Philip arriving in Jamaica on February 18, 2002. The couple was in Jamaica on a three-day visit, the first overseas trip of the Golden Jubilee to mark the Queen's 50th year as head of the British Monarchy and dependent territories.

Queen Elizabeth II inspects the guard of honour mounted by the First Battalion of the Jamaica Regiment at the Norman Manley International Airport after her arrival in Jamaica on February 18, 2002.

Terry-Ann James, a six-year-old student at the St. Simon's Basic school in Jones Town, shows Queen Elizabeth II the name of her school printed on the sign she is holding during Her Majesty's visit to the Hugh Sherlock Complex in Rema, South St. Andrew, on February 19, 2002.

Queen Elizabeth II accompanied by His Royal Highness, Prince Philip, braved a sudden downpour as she makes her way to lay a wreath at the cenotaph at National Heroes Park in Kingston on February 18, 2002. The royal couple is flanked by Governor-General, Sir Howard Cooke, government officials, among them Prime Minister PJ Patterson, Local Government Minister Arnold Bertram and Mayor of Kingston, Marie Atkins, and former head of the JDF, Major General Robert Neish.

Portia Simpson Miller Sworn in as First Female PM

2006

CONGRATULATIONS CALABAR – TVJ SCHOOLS' CHALLENGE CHAMPIONS 2006

CEFIRO NISSAN

The Gleaner

ESTABLISHED 1834

CEFIRO NISSAN

www.jamaica-gleaner.com | VOLUME 172 NO. 80 | FRIDAY, MARCH 31, 2006 | KINGSTON, JAMAICA | 70 PAGES | INCLUDES GCT $25

Madam PM

RUDOLPH BROWN/CHIEF PHOTOGRAPHER

Portia Simpson Miller raises the Bible as she takes the oath of office at her swearing-in ceremony as Prime Minister at King's House yesterday. Mrs. Simpson Miller, who succeeds P.J. Patterson, is the first woman to hold the office of Prime Minister of Jamaica. Looking on is Governor-General Professor Kenneth Hall.

Portia sworn in as Jamaica's first female head of Government

Petrina Francis
Staff Reporter

PORTIA SIMPSON Miller yesterday wrote a page in Jamaica's history by becoming the nation's first female Prime Minister, pledging to stamp out corruption, extortion and break the power of criminals.

Mrs. Simpson Miller also promised to advance human rights and individual liberty.

In the run-up to the special delegates' conference to elect a new Prime Minister in February, Mrs. Simpson Miller was harshly criticised by many who said she did not "match up" to her fellow contenders who all had the title of Doctor before their names.

But yesterday she said everyone was equal and should be treated as such.

"Each individual is sacred. None is more important than the other. Money should not make one person more important than the other, learning should not make one person more important ... nor should class, colour or gender. We are all equal ..." the new Prime Minister said to tumultuous applause.

COLOURFUL CEREMONY

In the colourful ceremony held on the lawns of King's House, St. Andrew, and watched by an estimated 10,000 guests and thousands more at home and abroad, Mrs. Simpson Miller also pledged to foster and facilitate conditions for employment and wealth creation.

She succeeds P.J. Patterson who stepped into retirement yesterday as the nation's longest-serving Prime Minister.

Adorned in an ivory skirt suit, trimmed with gold, Mrs. Simpson Miller told the gathering, which included Louis Farrakhan, head of the Nation of Islam, regional leaders, members from the United States Congress and others, that the state has a responsibility to protect the society.

"We cannot build the harmony and peace that this society so desperately needs unless all Jamaicans know that they will be treated with dignity and respect," she said.

She continued: "I pledge to ensure that the interests of all our people are protected, and that victimisation never rears its ugly head in any way under my administration."

The new Prime Minister takes up the mantle

Please see HISTORY, A3

A2: Get a glimpse of the day's events through our photo essay.

A3: International delegates offer congratulations and comment on Portia Simpson Miller's move into office.

A3: First things to do as new PM.

A3: This seat taken! No place for Opposition Leader Bruce Golding at swearing-in.

A4: Vox pop: What should Portia tackle first? The poll speaks

EDITORIAL	A8	MEMORIAM	B13
LETTERS	A9	ENTERTAINMENT	C1
WEATHER	A9	COMICS	C3
SPORT	B1	PUZZLES	C3
CARIBBEAN	B8	HOROSCOPE	C4
INTERNATIONAL	B9	MOVIES	C5
CLASSIFIED	B11	SOCIAL	D1

Prime Minister Portia Simpson Miller and her husband Errald Miller make their way down the steps of King's House on March 30, 2006.

Prime Minister Portia Simpson Miller accepts her Instrument of Appointment from Governor-General Professor Kenneth Hall during her swearing-in as the nation's first female prime minister at King's House on March 30, 2006.

A section of the large crowd at the swearing-in ceremony for Jamaica's first female prime minister, Portia Simpson Miller on March 30, 2006.

Nation of Islam head, Minister Louis Farrakhan, enters King's House yesterday along with his entourage to witness the swearing-in ceremony of Jamaica's first female prime minister, Portia Simpson Miller on March 30, 2006.

Scores of motorists christen toll gates

Tyrone Reid
Staff Reporter

A TOYOTA Hiace with a commercial licence plate number was the first vehicle to christen the toll gates at the Portmore leg of Highway 2000 yesterday morning.

The male driver, who was coming from the Corporate Area and heading into Portmore, drove through the toll gates about 9:37 a.m. sporting a toothy grin, as he sped off into the expanse of new road.

At about 9:53 a.m, licence number 5911 DX, another Toyota Hiace, was the maiden vehicle through the toll gates which are designated for vehicles heading from Portmore into the Corporate Area.

However, contrary to the toothy grin sported by her male counterpart, the female driver who christened the Portmore to Corporate Area toll gates was livid, as the timing of the opening of the toll gates caught her off guard.

"Upset! Pissed! I had to pay a $100 a while ago," she fumed "I never remembered, had I remembered I would not have driven here," she protested.

The female motorist, who resides in Mount Royal Estate, Portmore, told **The Sunday Gleaner** that she is numbered among the many residents who have pledged their support to a total boycott of the toll road until the Government reduces the toll to $30.

While scores of motorists lined up to use the toll gates, others were seen reversing and heading in the opposite direction in protest of the toll rates. The construction workers had to remove the barricades and make way for the motorists. Others were simply caught in the dragnet and just had to pay the toll to use the thoroughfare.

MOTORISTS DIVERTED

This happened because the toll gates were not opened until around 10 a.m., so motorists, thinking that they could still use the slip road and bypass the toll gates, were suddenly diverted to the toll plaza.

One stone-faced looking man told **The Sunday Gleaner** that he was caught between a rock and a hard place and was forced to use the toll road. "I live in Portmore, but I am late and that is why I am using it," explained the motorist, who was visibly upset.

Meantime, Yvonne McCormack, chairperson for the Portmore Citizens' Advisory Council was encouraged about the first day of the planned boycott.

"Well, I am very heartened. When I came on Mandela, there was a good amount of traffic so I take it to mean that people are using the alternate route," she said.

While scores of motorists lined up to use the toll gates, others were seen reversing and heading in the opposite direction in protest of the toll rates. The construction workers had to remove the barricades and make way for the motorists.

OUTSTANDING ADVISOR FOR JUNE 2008
Adassa Clahar
Sagicor
Wise Financial Thinking for Life
Knutsford Branch
Tel.: (876) 929-6820

The Sunday Gleaner

NEWS

Jamaica on storm watch

The Meteorological Service yesterday advised the Office of Disaster Preparedness and Emergency Management that the island was on a tropical storm watch, as weather conditions associated with Fay were expected to affect the island.

Injunction stops demolition plans

The Supreme Court has put the brakes on plans by the Kingston and St Andrew Corporation to demolish a building at 14 Caledonia Avenue in Cross Roads, St Andrew. That was after attorney-at-law Abe Dabdoub turned up with a court injunction putting a stop on the demolition.

GB (UK): £3.50, CAN: $4.95+GST, NY: $3.50, FLORIDA: $3.50

www.jamaica-gleaner.com VOLUME 69 NO. 33 AUGUST 17, 2008 KINGSTON, JAMAICA 138 PAGES INCLUDING GCT $100

SUPER BOLT

AP PHOTOS

Usain Bolt created Olympic history for Jamaica as he streaked to the gold medal in the 100m final yesterday. **SEE STORY ON B1**

CELEBRATE!
Scream! Shout! Jump!

SPORTS: B3
Women poised to strike

B2
Get all the times, results, standings

It's a People thing!
Jamaica's Credit Unions ...the POWER of PEOPLE

2008

www.jamaica-gleaner.com VOLUME 174 NO. 200 THURSDAY, AUGUST 21, 2008 KINGSTON, JAMAICA 56 PAGES INCLUDING GCT $30

Cool your Home for Less SINGER AT HOME WORLDWIDE

SALUTING OUR ATHLETES

The Gleaner

Big SAVINGS on Air Conditioning SINGER AT HOME WORLDWIDE

SMASHING

Melaine breaks Hemmings' Games record

BOLT shatters 200m world mark

MORE INSIDE

A3: Respect, Melaine!

A4: Golden bashment to welcome athletes

B1: 9.69 + 19.30 = History

C10: Sherwood 'Content' with Bolt

D6: Best wishes, Usain

FINANCIAL GLEANER: JPS'S MONTHLY $4-BILLION BURDEN • RIO BUENO GETS FIRST CARGO SHIP CALL

The Gleaner

...ANY DAY... ANY POLL... WE ARE NUMBER 1

www.jamaica-gleaner.com VOLUME 174 NO. 201 FRIDAY, AUGUST 22, 2008 KINGSTON, JAMAICA 74 PAGES INCLUDING GCT $30

NAVARA
NISSAN

Sweet repeat

Ver successfully defends 200m title

VERONICA CAMPBELL-BROWN yesterday took the 200-metre gold in Beijing, China, completing a Jamaican sweep of the sprint events at the 2008 Olympics and posting the seventh-fastest time ever and the fastest of the year.

Full story>>
B3: Gold number three for VCB

PHOTOS BY AP AND CHARLES PITT

Jamaican athletes (from top, left) Kerron Stewart, Veronica Campbell-Brown, Melaine Walker and Usain Bolt display their medals at the 2008 Olympics in Beijing, China, yesterday.

AP

Right: Jamaica's Veronica Campbell-Brown wins the gold medal in the women's 200-metre final in the National Stadium at the Beijing 2008 Olympics yesterday.

EDITORIAL	A8	ENTERTAINMENT	C1
OPINION	A9	MOVIES	C3
SPORTS	B1	COMICS	C9
CLASSIFIEDS	B13	HOROSCOPE	C10
MEMORIAM	B15	SOCIAL	D1

Olympic stories>>
A2: Family in Angels thanks God for Veronica's win
A3: 'Brand Bolt'
A10: Churchmen view the Games

OUTSTANDING ADVISOR FOR JULY 2008

Walter Grant SLU

Sagicor

Wise Financial Thinking for Life

Liguanea Branch

Tel.: (876) 383-7149

The Sunday Gleaner

ENTERTAINMENT

'Saving Grace' relocates dancehall

The New York-based actor/director Orville Matherson shows foreigners the brighter side of dancehall in 'Saving Grace', his low-budget film currently in production.

GB (UK): £3.50, CAN: $4.95+GST, NY: $3.50, FLORIDA: $3.50

www.jamaica-gleaner.com VOLUME 69 NO. 34 AUGUST 24, 2008 KINGSTON, JAMAICA 156 PAGES INCLUDING GCT $100

GREAT HAUL OF CHINA

Ja's record-breaking Olympic performance

Elton Tucker
Assistant Sport Editor

BEIJING:

JAMAICA ENDED a record-breaking medal performance at the 2008 Olympic Games with a bronze in the women's 4x400 metres on the final day of competition for the nation's athletes at the Bird's Nest Stadium in Beijing yesterday.

The island's contingent here, led by an awesome performance from Usain Bolt, finished with a record 11 medals – six gold, three silver and two bronze – beating, by four, the previous highest tally of seven at the Sydney Games in 2000.

Jamaica had never won more than two gold medals at any one Games before. This time, they captured three times as many to finish third on the track-and-field table, behind powerhouses United States with seven gold, nine silver and seven bronze, and Russia with six gold, five silver and seven bronze.

Overall, with all its medals coming in track and field, Jamaica placed 13th. Hosts China are in an unassailable lead with 49 gold, 19 silver and 28 bronze with one day to go. The United States have the most medals – 107 – comprising 34 gold, 37 silver and 36 bronze.

Bolt was the star of the show. He is the second man to win three gold medals in athletics at the same Games since 1956. American Carl Lewis won four gold medals at Los Angeles in 1984.

The 22-year-old Jamaican sprint sensation is also the 14th man to win at least three gold medals in a single Games after capturing gold medals in 100m, 200m and 4x100m, all in world-record times.

See Olympic wrap-up on B3

KFC
LET'S BUCKET TOGETHER
FAMILY 12
12 pieces of chicken
1 family fries
4 biscuits
3 coleslaws
3 mashed potatoes
4 cookies
1 Pepsi 2L
KFC
Proud Sponsor of
JAMAICA 60
Re-igniting a Nation for Greatness
Limited Time Offer. Conditions Apply. Visuals shows are representational.

The Indomitable Spirit of the Jamaican Woman

Senator Janice S. Allen

Having been raised by and around women who make things move, who get things done, I can't help but acknowledge and recognise the Spirit of the Jamaican woman *as we celebrate our 60th year of Independence as a nation. All of us as Jamaicans can testify to the influence of a strong Jamaican woman in our lives. Our mothers, grandmothers, aunts, the teacher or vendor, the household worker. I know of no Jamaican who can honestly say they are not the beneficiary of a strong Jamaican woman in their life. There is no doubt that when you have a Jamaican woman in your corner, defending you, supporting and encouraging you, there is nothing you can't achieve.*

My mother, for example, has instilled within my sister and me the value of hard work and that nothing is too little to take on and nothing is too big to attempt. It is because of her (even though my father was always there) that we approach life the way we do. She always says, "Whatever it is, go for it as you have nothing to lose" and "ask for anything you want because there are only two possible answers, yes or no, so ask because you never know, you might just get what you want." It is because of her example on a daily basis that maybe I am not easily impressed by anything or anyone because what she has taught me is that I can do anything and still be humble, caring and ambitious all at once.

I know my mother is no different from many other mothers in Jamaica. I see them every day and I am sure I will go unchallenged in my assessment. I see them, especially during these difficult times, dealing with the effects of the pandemic, managing their households, many as single mothers, ensuring their children's education is taken care of even when they themselves might not be at the same level of education as their children. I see them hustling in the markets to sell their goods to feed their children and also to advance their own education to achieve their dream. I see the household helper who, on minimum wage and a constant partner plan, is still able to send her children to school and produce some of Jamaica's best in various fields whether agriculture, medicine, law or business.

Our communities have at their cornerstone, women who are risk-takers, care-givers, peace-makers and game -changers. Just recently I had a conversation with an American who was trying to describe to me the personality of a woman born in the United States whom he does business with, as "she could be a Jamaican woman". He was describing for me a no-nonsense woman in business who had clearly made him understand that she knew what she wanted and was not going to be stopped by him or any other from getting what she had set her eyes on. This is the perfect description of a Jamaican woman as there is very little we are daunted by and very little that will make us cower. The true Jamaican woman is certain, confident and assured, and will be stopped by no one or stop at nothing especially for her children and definitely knows how to make something from nothing – *'tek her han tun fashion'!*

In this our 60th year, I want to acknowledge the spirit of the Jamaican woman as she captures for me everything that makes the best of Jamaica. It is on the backs of women that our great nation has been able to get to where it is today. It is because of this spirit why we have so many amazing women in leadership, whether in the private or the public sector, heading households, or heading up their own small- and medium-sized businesses. Women leading corporations, service organizations, women in politics.

As we celebrate we must further support because many women today still need to be supported in various ways in order for them to reach their full potential. Financial independence and literacy is an area where if more of our women were exposed to from an early age we would probably see more women achieve greater. We must ensure that the legislative structure of our country is such that is provides greater platform for women to enter into and thrive in other capacities. As we turn 60 we must recommit as a nation to ensuring that we mentor more, support more and provide more for women because a society that does this goes beyond expectations.

Everywhere in the world we go we see our Jamaican women leading the charge and changing the world in science, medicine, business, education, philanthropy, politics, in every area. Therefore, in this our 60th year of Independence, I celebrate the *indomitable spirit of the Jamaican woman* as she proves to be the epitome of what is the *Best of Jamaica!*

Senator Janice Allen is Opposition Spokesperson on Tourism and a Business Development Consultant.

Commitment to Country

Peter Melhado

In a developing country, I believe that people typically hanker for what pertains in more developed societies and over time that yearning forms a national dialogue dominated by cynicism and resignation, with bright spots treated as anomalous and ephemeral. I would posit that the grass is always greener on the 'other side' and that Jamaica, despite its many problems, remains a country of genuine souls who regularly support one another in overcoming hardships, especially at the level of community. Our challenge then is to translate these results to the national stage. An accumulation of such outcomes would shift our context towards confidence and capacity, and empower us as a nation to achieve great things.

To this end, one such national quality that stands out and bears nurturing is our commitment to country and by extension, to one another. If harnessed effectively, this quality can become a key lever in generating the shift from passive participants in a downward spiral to active contributors in nation-building.

For me a recent manifestation of this quality was Jamaica's response to the COVID-19 pandemic. In writing this, I can already hear many of my colleagues snickering, no doubt thinking that my hypothesis and the actual results are diametrically opposed and that I have become addled by drinking Kool Aid of a certain variety. So let me state my case not from a verandah chair, but from being deeply engaged with the many problems faced over a protracted period of time in fighting the pandemic. I became involved with the pandemic response effort in March 2021, when I joined the Private Sector Vaccine Initiative, formed by a committed group of Jamaicans. The entity's mission was to lend support to the government in its efforts to procure and deliver vaccinations at a time when the global supply was constrained. Our first task was to assist the Ministry of Health and Wellness in preparing to receive its first shipments of vaccines and ensuring our health system could collect and manage inoculation data in an efficient manner.

It is common knowledge that the public sector has certain rigidities in its design, including protracted decision-making cycles with many layers of checks and balances. In order to work together, both sides had to meet in the middle and as we went about building mutual trust and credibility, commitment to nation was the common ground we came back to time and again.

It is easy to forget that the ministry team had been managing the first waves of the outbreak for over 12 months before vaccines became available; frontline workers were risking their lives day in and day out, and the administrative teams were stretched managing policy formulation, logistics planning and people. Despite this, from the minister down, the team was willing to engage, listen and adapt valid suggestions.

It was an intense period as we sought to source and localise software with limited options given the recent existence of the pandemic and the lack of developed solutions that would fit our agreed criteria. Commitment to nation was again apparent as everyone I asked to serve on the evaluation panel unhesitatingly raised their hand, regardless of their schedule, and on one basis, Jamaica needed them. Many late nights and weekends later, we achieved an open-source solution that has recorded over one million vaccination events to date, against all odds and within the very narrow time-frame required.

Looking back, I have also reflected on the participation of a major multi-lateral (UNICEF) in the process. They have been invaluable partners throughout the journey by providing funding, technical support and plain old elbow grease when the going got tough. I have since become aware that a compelling reason for their involvement was the nexus of public and private sectors, working together with the common goal of national improvement. In fact, my good friends at UNICEF have arranged a symposium to study the galvanising effects of stakeholder partnerships in advancing national efforts, shorthand for how love of country and its corollary, commitment, can make a positive difference.

Coming back to my original thesis, time and again, whether it be EPOC or this example, Jamaicans have come together in commitment to their country and delivered on their mission. In a small country with limited resources, harnessing everyone's commitment can be colossal. Too often, in my view, we get distracted by small differences that hide the bigger picture, sabotaging our ability to build on past efforts and bringing a negative quality to our national discourse. If I can wish one thing, it is that we can put these things aside and create a highway of collaboration that, over time, can replace resignation with hope for the future of our beloved Jamaica.

Peter Melhado is the President and Chief Executive Officer of the ICD Group and Chairman of Sagicor Investments Jamaica Limited.

Out of Many, One

Sheila Benjamin

Passionate, selfless, diverse, and vibrant are just a few of the words that appear with each thought of what it means to be Jamaican. To an immeasurable extent, these words illustrate the undying spirit of survival that has moulded our country into the prosperous island gem it is today. But perhaps the expression that most fittingly describes the authentic Jamaican experience is resilience. And no other aspect of our beloved motherland better emulates this quality than the Jamaican people themselves.

Exemplified by a recurrent demonstration of our ability to thrive through hardship and emerge stronger and wiser than before, our people's resilience continually shines atop seemingly insurmountable challenges. Every year, Jamaica's natural susceptibility to the raw elements of nature is recurrently realized. We brace for impact at the dawn of the annual hurricane season, and no year is ever short of torrents. Time and time, again, our geographical predilections render the livelihoods of thousands of Jamaicans, particularly farmers, vulnerable to the occasionally mild, often devastating effects of turbulent weather conditions. But no storm, either natural or otherwise, has managed to raze and subjugate our people for long. Driven by our need to thrive, bolstered by our inherent will to survive, our people arise from every storm and blossom with renewed purpose.

Our resilience doesn't stop at our ability to bounce back from devasting showers and gales. In recent times, we've seen first-hand how that remarkable quality can transcend unprecedented challenges, bringing us all closer together. The rise of COVID-19 and the subsequent pandemic placed the world in a choke-hold. No sector or industry has escaped the damaging impact. Closer to home, our children were perhaps one of the most significantly impacted demographics as the pandemic forced them out of their classrooms and into their homes. The discontinuation of face-to-face classes left many students without any means to continue their education. But it didn't take long for us to launch a response where private and public sector agencies and individuals alike spearheaded the establishment of various Internet access points across the island. We realised the need for our children to maintain access to their education, and together, we ventured to support the most underserved of them all. By no small measure, these efforts have uplifted many lives and have helped to safeguard a vulnerable generation rich with promise, potential, and talent.

The range of talents that Jamaica nurtures and releases into the diaspora spans various sectors and industries. The achievements of many of our musicians and athletes have made them household names, and our people's extensive influence continues to surge beyond barriers. Our prongs have recently stretched and left another indelible mark at the Winter Olympics, where our tropical island saw its first representative in the highly technical alpine skiing discipline. Our 1988 Winter Games debut in the bobsledding event is a memory shared throughout households. The addition of another competition to our not-so-tropical repertoire only harps on our enduring crusade to spread our wings as wide as the horizon stretches. A common question that surfaces when we think of the reach and accomplishments of our people is just how far across the world is Jamaica's presence felt? But the world is not as big as it seems when we stop to think. Where in the world can't we find a Jamaican? Time after time, our resonating presence bolsters our culture's undying flame through music, cuisine, sport, and a spectrum of engagements that keep us on the minds of our global neighbours.

Our people sustain and embrace our country's cultural diversity, creating a homeland that is as accommodating to visitors as it is to the various ancestries that make us out of many, one. The story of the Guardsman Group embodies our people's welcoming spirit and emphasizes Jamaica's rank as a place of refuge for many and a home for all. Kenneth Sushil Benjamin, the pioneer and game-changer behind the Guardsman Group, couldn't have imagined just how much the people of this once-upon-a-time foreign land would help transform his life. After arriving on the island in 1972, Benjamin slowly paved a path that would lead to the establishment of Jamaica's premier security company. By the time his dream had come to fruition, however, the impact of our nation's nurturing inhabitants had captured his heart and soul, rendering him immovable. Years of living, studying, working, and thriving among the people of our beloved country left no doubt in Benjamin's mind that Jamaica would be his new home. Today, the Guardsman Group flourishes on the shoulders of a staff cohort as diverse as the company itself. Guardsman continues to succeed and expand thanks to the passionate, selfless, resilient, and talented people who built it from the ground up and continue to make it a leader in its field, the people of Jamaica.

Sheila Benjamin is Director of Guardsman Group Limited.

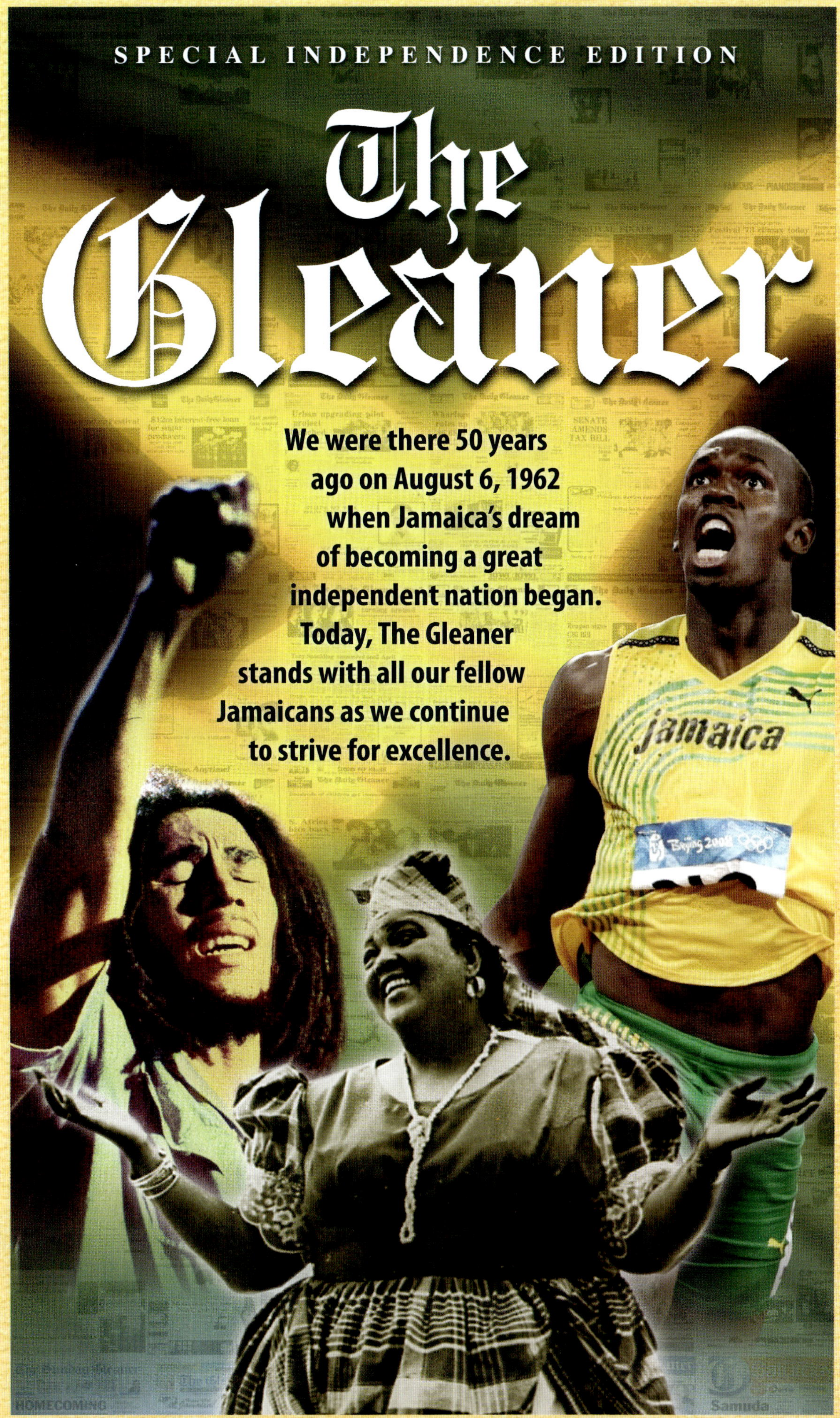
SPECIAL INDEPENDENCE EDITION
The Gleaner
We were there 50 years ago on August 6, 1962 when Jamaica's dream of becoming a great independent nation began. Today, The Gleaner stands with all our fellow Jamaicans as we continue to strive for excellence.
jamaica
Beijing 2008

Mello Go Roun concert, held at Jamaica 50 Golden Jubilee Village, Independence Park, on Thursday night August 2, 2012.

Members of uniformed groups stand at attention for the national anthem at the start of the Independence Grand Gala.

Dignitaries in the Royal Box at the Independence Grand Gala at the National Stadium on August 6, 2012. From left are: Kingston Mayor Angela Brown Burke; Prime Minister Portia Simpson Miller; General Colin Powell; CARICOM Secretary-General Irwin LaRocque; and South African President Jacob Zuma and his wife, Nompumelelo Mantuli.

Several people dressed in black, green and gold at the 2012 Jamaica 50 Golden Jubilee Village, Independence Park during the celebrations.

A section of the Grandstand at the National Stadium for the 2012 Independence Grand Gala.

www.jamaica-gleaner.com VOLUME 178 NO. 186 MONDAY, AUGUST 6, 2012 KINGSTON, JAMAICA 128 PAGES INCLUDING GCT $50

The Gleaner

YOUR NEWSPAPER S

HURRICANE Bolt

Usain, Yohan give Ja birthday gift

André Lowe
Senior Staff Reporter

LONDON, England:

ERNESTO MIGHT have spared Jamaica, for the most part, but the world felt the effects of 'Hurricane Bolt' when Jamaican superstar Usain Bolt successfully defended his Olympic 100m title, sprinting to an Olympic record 9.63, as Jamaica booked its third and fourth medals at these games – the perfect gift to a nation celebrating its 50th year of Independence today.

PLEASE SEE **BOLT**, A2

9.63
OLYMPIC RECORD

DAEGU LONDON JAMAICA'S JOURNEY
LONDON 2012

SCHEDULE OF EVENTS

TODAY

TIME	SEX	EVENT	ROUND
AFTERNOON SESSION			
1:00	W	Pole Vault	Final
1:15	W	Shot Put	Final
1:20	W	200 Metres	Heats
2:15	W	400 Metres Hurdles	Semi-Final
2:45	M	400 Metres Hurdles	Final
3:05	W	3000m Steeplechase	Final
3:30	M	400 Metres	Final

AUGUST 7

TIME	SEX	EVENT	ROUND
MORNING SESSION			
4:00	W	Javelin Throw	Qualification
4:10	M	110 Metres Hurdles	Heats
4:45	M	Triple Jump	Qualification
4:55	W	5000 Metres	Heats
5:25	W	Javelin Throw	Qualification
5:50	M	200 Metres	Heats
AFTERNOON SESSION			
1:00	M	High Jump	Final
1:05	W	Long Jump	Qualification
1:15	W	100 Metres Hurdles	Semi-Final
1:45	M	Discus Throw	Final
1:55	M	800 Metres	Semi-Final
2:25	W	200 Metres	Semi-Final
3:00	W	100 Metres Hurdles	Final
3:15	M	1500 Metres	Final

JAMAICAN DREAM A4
EDITORIAL A5
OPINION A6
SPORTS B1
HORSERACING B5
ENTERTAINMENT D1
MOVIES D3
COMICS D4
HOROSCOPE D5
CLASSIFIEDS D14
MEMORIAM C14

2012

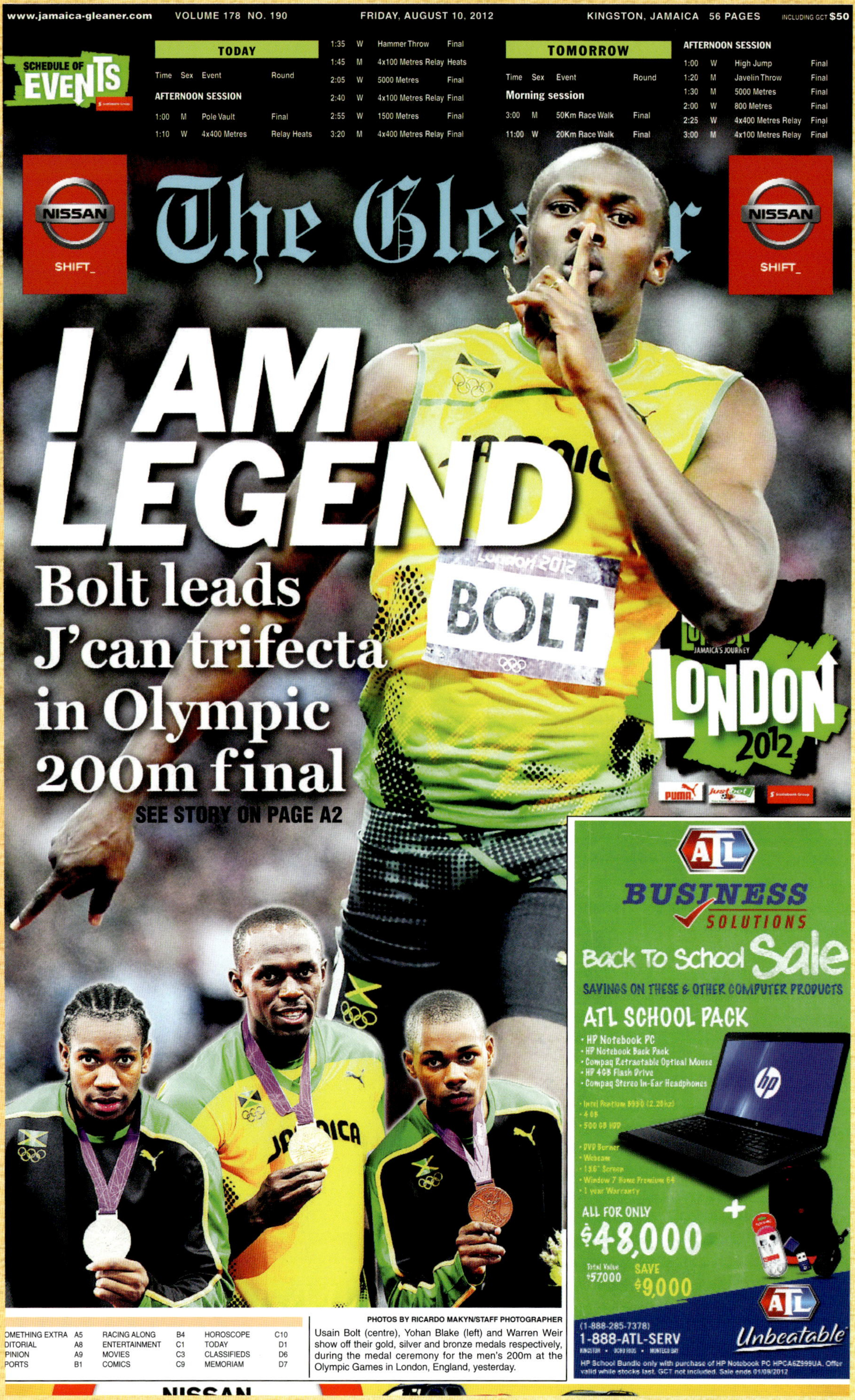

www.jamaica-gleaner.com VOLUME 178 NO. 190 FRIDAY, AUGUST 10, 2012 KINGSTON, JAMAICA 56 PAGES INCLUDING GCT $50

SCHEDULE OF EVENTS

TODAY

Time	Sex	Event	Round
AFTERNOON SESSION			
1:00	M	Pole Vault	Final
1:10	W	4x400 Metres	Relay Heats
1:35	W	Hammer Throw	Final
1:45	M	4x100 Metres Relay	Heats
2:05	W	5000 Metres	Final
2:40	W	4x100 Metres Relay	Final
2:55	W	1500 Metres	Final
3:20	M	4x400 Metres Relay	Final

TOMORROW

Time	Sex	Event	Round
Morning session			
3:00	M	50Km Race Walk	Final
11:00	W	20Km Race Walk	Final
AFTERNOON SESSION			
1:00	W	High Jump	Final
1:20	M	Javelin Throw	Final
1:30	M	5000 Metres	Final
2:00	W	800 Metres	Final
2:25	W	4x400 Metres Relay	Final
3:00	M	4x100 Metres Relay	Final

The Gleaner

I AM LEGEND

Bolt leads J'can trifecta in Olympic 200m final

SEE STORY ON PAGE A2

PHOTOS BY RICARDO MAKYN/STAFF PHOTOGRAPHER

Usain Bolt (centre), Yohan Blake (left) and Warren Weir show off their gold, silver and bronze medals respectively, during the medal ceremony for the men's 200m at the Olympic Games in London, England, yesterday.

OMETHING EXTRA	A5	RACING ALONG	B4	HOROSCOPE	C10
DITORIAL	A8	ENTERTAINMENT	C1	TODAY	D1
PINION	A9	MOVIES	C3	CLASSIFIEDS	D6
PORTS	B1	COMICS	C9	MEMORIAM	D7

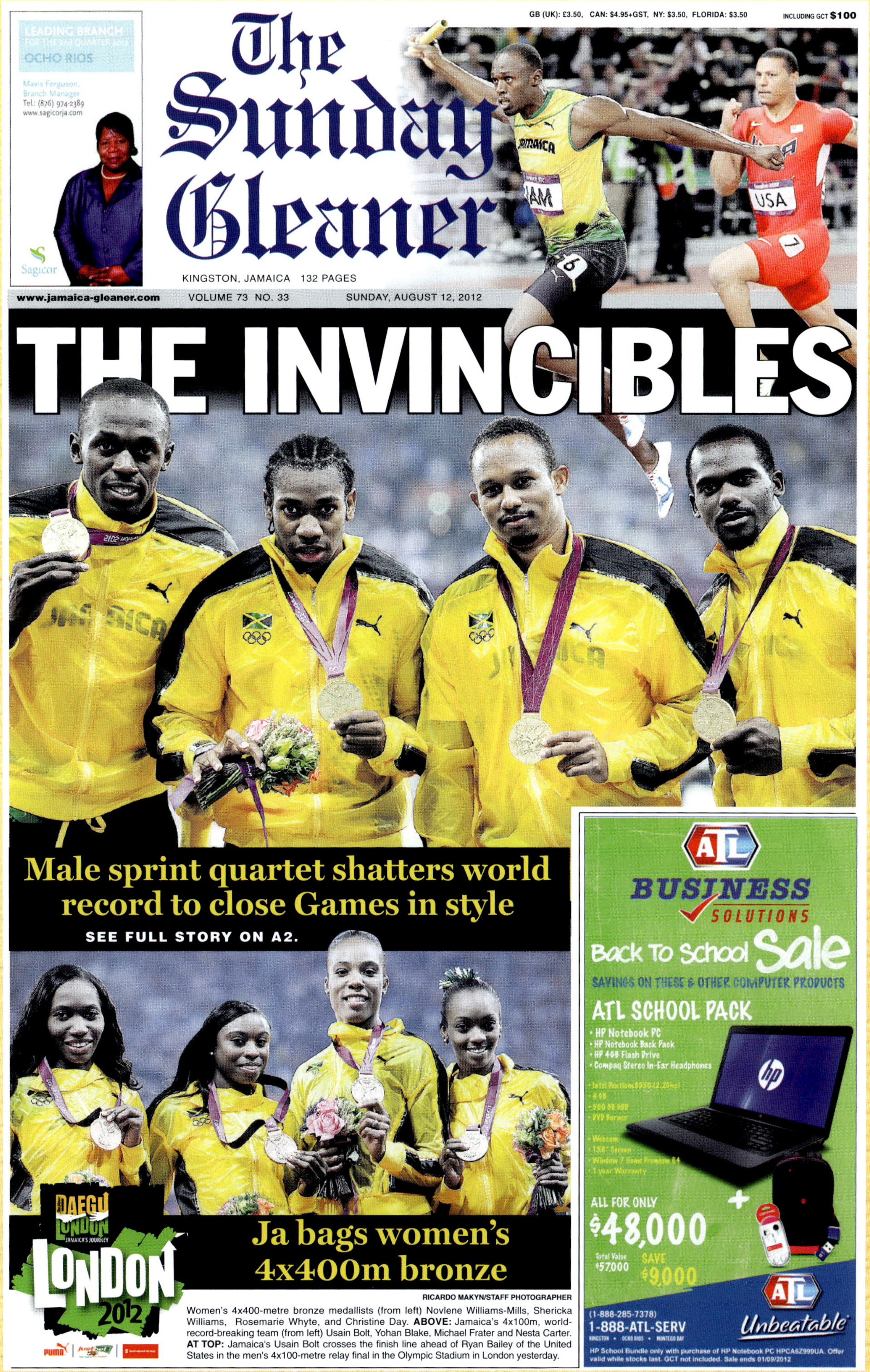
GB (UK): £3.50, CAN: $4.95+GST, NY: $3.50, FLORIDA: $3.50 INCLUDING GCT $100

The Sunday Gleaner

KINGSTON, JAMAICA 132 PAGES

www.jamaica-gleaner.com VOLUME 73 NO. 33 SUNDAY, AUGUST 12, 2012

THE INVINCIBLES

Male sprint quartet shatters world record to close Games in style

SEE FULL STORY ON A2.

Ja bags women's 4x400m bronze

DAEGU LONDON JAMAICA'S JOURNEY
LONDON 2012

RICARDO MAKYN/STAFF PHOTOGRAPHER

Women's 4x400-metre bronze medallists (from left) Novlene Williams-Mills, Shericka Williams, Rosemarie Whyte, and Christine Day. **ABOVE:** Jamaica's 4x100m, world-record-breaking team (from left) Usain Bolt, Yohan Blake, Michael Frater and Nesta Carter. **AT TOP:** Jamaica's Usain Bolt crosses the finish line ahead of Ryan Bailey of the United States in the men's 4x100-metre relay final in the Olympic Stadium in London yesterday.

Moscow World Champs

www.jamaica-gleaner.com VOLUME 179 NO. 196 KINGSTON, JAMAICA 32 PAGES INCLUDING GCT $50

The Gleaner
Saturday

AUGUST 17, 2013

FEATURES INSIDE

The Gleaner RURAL Xpress
Exposing The Extraordinary!

... SEE PAGES C1-4

The Gleaner's western FOCUS
NOT JUST NEWS ...YOUR NEWS

... SEE PAGES D1-4

Follow us on:
YouTube

Superwoman Shelly

'Pocket Rocket' lands historic sprint double with 200m gold at World Champs

RICARDO MAKYN/STAFF PHOTOGRAPHER

'Pocket Rocket' Shelly-Ann Fraser-Pryce celebrates with the Jamaica flag after sealing a historic sprint double with her 200-metre victory, at the World Championships of Athletics inside the Luzhniki Stadium, Moscow, yesterday. Fraser-Pryce had earlier won the 100 metres.

André Lowe
Senior Staff Reporter

MOSCOW, Russia:

JAMAICA ADDED two medals on yesterday's seventh day of competition at the IAAF World Championships in Athletics – one, a display of pure class; the other, a reward for courage, class, and determination.

Shelly-Ann Fraser-Pryce and the Javon Francis-powered men's 4x400m relay team turned the Luzhniki Stadium into a big Jamaican party, as waving flags and Bob Marley songs rocked the iconic Moscow landmark, as Jamaica celebrated its fourth and fifth medals here.

Fraser-Pryce became the first Jamaican woman and only the third in history to win the sprint double at the World Championships, adding her 200m title to the 100m gold won on Monday, with another commanding display.

The other two World Champs female double-sprint champions are Germans Silke Gladisch in 1987 and Katrin Krabbe in 1991.

The two medals won yesterday lifted

PLEASE SEE **SHELLY**, A3

PUMA MOSCOW SCHEDULE

Today

JA TIME	SEX	EVENT	ROUND
6:30 AM	M	Marathon	Final
9:00 AM	W	High Jump	Final
9:20 AM	W	100 Metres Hurdles	Semi-Final
		Danielle Williams, Shermaine Williams	
9:35 AM	M	Javelin Throw	Final
9:55 AM	W	5000 Metres	Final
10:30 AM	W	100 Metres Hurdles	Final
10:45 AM	W	4x400 Metres Relay	Final
		Jamaica disqualified	
11:10 AM	M	200 Metres	Final
		Usain Bolt, Warren Weir, Nickel Ashmeade	

'A blessing from God'

Mom sings praises after 100m-200m success

FILE

Shelly-Ann Fraser-Pryce's mother, Maxine Simpson (left) and grandmother, Phedalia Simpson.

Robert Bailey
Gleaner Writer

AN OVER-THE-MOON Maxine Simpson, mother of the newly crowned world sprint-double champion Shelly-Ann Fraser-Pryce, could hardly contain her joy after her daughter captured the women's 200m at the 14th IAAF World Championships in Athletics in Moscow, Russia, yesterday.

Simpson, as bubbly as her daughter, said she never doubted that Fraser-Pryce would have won yesterday's event because she is a firm believer in God.

"First thing, I have to give God thanks, because if it wasn't for that man, I don't know what would have happened and so I have to trust him," said Simpson.

"I said to myself before the start of the race that this is it, and when she was in the lane I said 'I give you my blessing girl', and when she lifted up then I saw the race done and she was in front," said an elated Simpson.

Fraser-Pryce, who on Monday won the 100m gold, returned to the track yesterday to clock 22.17 on her way to winning the 200m final.

HAD NO DOUBT

Simpson said she was very confident her daughter would have won the double at this year's championships.

"I had no doubt that she was going to win because of her times that she did in the heat and semi-final, and also the times that she ran in the 100m," said Simpson.

"I am happy and I feel good when I saw her crossing that line in front. I was in my room jumping up and down on the bed and shouting, 'Thank you Jesus, one more gold'," she said.

A thankful Simpson heaped more praises on God for the win she said brought her to tears.

"This one feels great," Simpson said. "Oh my God, when I saw her take that bend with her face made up, you could see the determination in her eyes," she said. "I feel so good, this is special to me and this is great to me. This is a blessing from God."

The 26-year-old Fraser-Pryce is also the Beijing 2008 and London 2012 Olympic 100m champion.

2013

MEET YOUR LIME-GLEANER

Inner-city overachiever

See Pages A3 & A8

Chevoy Craigie

Defying all odds to become a member of the 'Fab Five'. From Mico Practising Primary and Junior High School to Jamaica College

The Gleaner

THE LEADER IN CREDIBILITY

www.jamaica-gleaner.com VOLUME 179 NO. 197 MONDAY, AUGUST 19, 2013 KINGSTON, JAMAICA 52 PAGES INCLUDING GCT $50

DREAM SWEEP

BAILEY-COLE CARTER ASHMEADE BOLT STEWART FRASER-PRYCE RUSSELL CALVERT

Ja takes six sprint gold in nine-medal haul

André Lowe
Senior Staff Reporter

MOSCOW, Russia:

SHELLY-ANN Fraser-Pryce became the first Jamaican woman to win three gold medals at a senior championship and Usain Bolt also made it a trio of wins after Jamaica's 4x100m relay teams ended the IAAF World Championships with fireworks and a double gold-medal sweep at the Luzhniki Stadium in Moscow, Russia.

Bolt's third gold medal also ensured that he joins Carl Lewis as the male athlete with the most medals at the World Championships with 10.

Bolt also leads on quality with eight gold and two silver. Lewis has eight gold, a silver and a bronze.

Yesterday's results mean that the Jamaicans will leave Moscow with nine medals: six gold – their second-highest

PLEASE SEE **SWEEP**, A3

FRASER-PRYCE

BOLT

PHOTOS BY RICARDO MAKYN/STAFF PHOTOGRAPHER

"I was thinking that I am not a very good anchor ... but it was wonderful and I enjoyed it."

"I wasn't worried, I knew my team would be great ... I have to give thanks to the guys. They came out and ran well for the team."

OPERATION MOSCOW

IAAF WORLD CHAMPIONSHIPS IN ATHLETICS 2013

See more coverage on Pages A3, A4 and in Section B.

Jamaicans (from left) Shelly-Ann Fraser-Pryce, Kerron Stewart, Schillonie Calvert and Carrie Russell celebrate with the national flag after winning the women's 4x100 metres relay at the Luzhniki Stadium, at the 2013 World Championships in Athletics in Moscow, Russia in August 2013.

www.jamaica-gleaner.com VOLUME 181 NO. 85 FRIDAY, APRIL 10, 2015 KINGSTON, JAMAICA 64 PAGES INCLUDING GCT $60

The Gleaner 180

Years for You

THE LEADER IN CRE[...]ILITY

OBAMA

1,313 MINUTES IN PARADISE

US PRESIDENT ANNOUNCES US$70M YOUTH INITIATIVE: A3

CONGRESSWOMAN CLARKE: A SENSE OF PRIDE SWELL UP INSIDE MY CHEST: A2

2015

The Gleaner 180

THE LEADER IN CREDIBILITY

Years for You

KINGSTON, JAMAICA 62 PAGES

www.jamaica-gleaner.com VOL 181 NO. 84 THURSDAY, APRIL 9, 2015 INCLUDING GCT $60

OBAMA ON THE ROCK!

RICARDO MAKYN/ STAFF PHOTOGRAPHER

United States President Barack Obama waves as he alights from Air Force One at the Norman Manley International Airport in Kingston last night. Behind him is Congresswoman Yvette Clarke.

Anastasia Cunningham
News Coordinator

AN UNSCHEDULED visit to the Bob Marley Museum by United States President Barack Obama took most persons by surprise. After landing in Jamaica last night, the president had a yearning to enjoy a bit of Jamaica's warmth, colour, culture and beauty before delving into the official nature of his first visit to the island.

See full story on A3.

OBAMA ON THE ROCK

CHECK OUT THESE VIDEOS ONLINE AT WWW.JAMAICA-GLEANER.COM/VIDEOS

SAY WELCOME TO BARACK — ERICA'S EDGE

THE 'OBAMA' INTERVIEW — MR PRESIDENT …

PICTURE THIS

SEE SECTION E FOR OUR SPECIAL FEATURE MARKING THE PRESIDENT'S VISIT.

US President Barrack Obama (right) meets with World War 11 veteran Colonel Torrance Lewis just before he laid a wreath at National Heroes Park on Thursday, April 9, 2015. Looking on are World War II veterans Barry Beckford and Major Victor Beek.

US$5m being sought for J'can villa
See Page 7

The Weekly GLEANER with EXTRA NA
EXTRA NORTH AMERICA
www.jamaica-gleaner.com

www.jamaica-gleaner.com VOLUME 2227 | 28 PAGES DECEMBER 31, 2015, JANUARY 6, 2016 US$1.2

JAMAICA STOCK EXCHANGE IS ON TOP OF THE WORLD

The Jamaica Stock Exchange at Harbour Street, Kingston.

AMID THE middling returns of the world's best known indexes - foreign acquisitions, stronger investor safeguards and a rebounding economy helped the Jamaica Stock Exchange (JSE) surge more than 80 percent in 2015, reported Bloomberg News, a run that has impressed analysts globally.

"I think it reflects a very good development and certainly should provide impetus for capital raising by companies, and, hopefully, will prompt other companies to list on the stock market over time," said Finance Minister Peter Phillips.

Please see STOCK, 3

Peter Phillips

Road deaths set to become second highest in a decade | Story on PAGE 3

Golden Krust
TRY OUR NEW!
Curry Mutton Patty
Limited Time Offer At Participating Locations
www.goldenkrustbakery.com 718-OK-KRUST
370 Calories

2015

TOP LEFT: Mexico's head coach Miguel Herrera.

TOP CENTRE: Reggae Boyz Joel McAnuff (left), Rodolph Austin (centre) and Je-Vaughn Watson celebrate after qualifying for today's Gold Cup final.

TOP RIGHT: Jamaica's head coach Winfried Schäfer.

BOTTOM: Reggae Boy Simon Dawkins.

PRICE INCREASE

…ease note that effective August 2, 2015, the price of **The Sunday Gleaner** will be increased to $140. This has become necessary in … face of rising input costs and we urge your understanding. We commit to continue producing products of the highest quality and …edibility for our readers and advertisers.

2015

www.jamaica-gleaner.com VOLUME 182 NO. 48 THURSDAY, FEBRUARY 25, 2016 KINGSTON, JAMAICA 40 PAGES INCLUDING GCT $60

Safe Food

The Gleaner

Safe Food

JAMAICA VOTES

SHOWDOWN!

CANDIDATES HOURS AWAY FROM FINISH LINE

Gary Spaulding
Senior Gleaner Writer

AFTER AN eventful political campaign that intensified over the last two weeks, an epic electoral contest looms large today on the country's colourful political landscape.

As the Electoral Office of Jamaica (EOJ) pronounced its readiness, the much-anticipated showdown between the People's National Party (PNP) and the Jamaica Labour Party (JLP) is rushing to its climax.

With both major parties in a statistical dead heat, anticipation is high as Jamaicans head to voting booths across the island.

JLP leader Andrew Holness is hoping to upstage PNP President

PLEASE SEE **VOTES**, A3

JLP leader Andrew Holness and PNP President Portia Simpson Miller have both expressed confidence ahead of today's polls.

2016

www.jamaica-gleaner.com VOLUME 182 NO. 49 FRIDAY, FEBRUARY 26, 2016 KINGSTON, JAMAICA 68 PAGES INCLUDING GCT $60

>> C11: TUFTON, MONTAGUE RETURN TO THE HOUSE

The Gleaner

JLP's prosperity message trumps ruling party

JA GOES GREEN

JAMAICA VOTES 2016

The Jamaica Labour Party (JLP) has rebounded from a turbulent four years to defy great political odds and seize the win in the nation's 17th general election. When the dust settled after an incident-filled day, the JLP secured more than 12 marginal seats to move past the much-needed 32 seats to form the next Government.

See full story on A3>>

THE NEW PARLIAMENT:

52 MEN 11 WOMEN

>>GUESS WHAT:

OF FOUR GENERAL ELECTIONS HELD IN FEBRUARY, THE JLP HAS WON TWO

OF THE 17 BATTLEGROUND SEATS:

St Elizabeth South Western; St James Central; Clarendon North Central; Clarendon South Eastern; St Mary Western; St Andrew East Rural; St Andrew Eastern; St Andrew West Rural; St James East Central; St James West Central; St Catherine East Central; Hanover Eastern; St Thomas Western; St Ann South Western; St Catherine North Eastern 15

Manchester Central; St Thomas Eastern 2

12 SEATS SWITCHED TO JLP

DISTRIBUTION OF SEATS

2016

2011

Jamaica at the Rio Olympics

www.jamaica-gleaner.com VOLUME 182 NO. 194 MONDAY, AUGUST 15, 2016 KINGSTON, JAMAICA 48 PAGES INCLUDING GCT $60

FRUIT JAZZ PUNCHES

THE LEADER … LITY

"I came here to show the world again that I am the best, and this is a good start."

Rio GOLD RUSH

COVERAGE BROUGHT TO YOU BY: FLOW JN PUMA

THE GREATEST

VICTORIOUS BOLT SPRINTS TO HISTORIC THIRD OLYMPIC 100M TITLE

SEE STORY ON PAGE A2

	100M	200M	4X100
2008	●	●	●
2012	●	●	●
2016	●		

Rio SCHEDULE JN

7:30 am – Men's triple jump qualifying
Clive Pullen
7:35 am – Women's 200m rd 1
Elaine Thompson, Veronica Campbell-Brown, Simone Facey
9:15 am – Women's 3000m Steeplechase final
Aisha Praugh
9:35 am – Men's 400m Hurdles rd 1
Roxroy Cato, Jaheel Hyde, Annsert Whyte
1:15 pm – Men's 3m Springboard prelim
Yona Knight-Wisdom
6:30 pm – Women's discus throw
Shadae Lawrence
Tarasue Barnett
Kellion Knibb
6:40 pm – Men's 110m hurdles rd1
Omar McLeod
Deuce Carter
Andrew Riley
7:30 pm – Women's 400m hurdles rd 1
Janieve Russell
Leah Nugent
Risatanna Tracey
8:45 pm – Women's 400m final
Stephenie McPherson
Shericka Jackson

FLOW Rio STARS

OMAR MCLEOD

The favourite in the men's 110m hurdles takes to the track today to begin his quest for Olympic gold.

2016

FLOW Rio STARS

Elaine Thompson

Elaine Thompson, Jamaica's and the world's new sprint queen, is poised for more glory at 8:15 tonight in Rio. She will be hunting the triple when Jamaica takes on the United States in the sprint relay. Thompson could become the first Jamaican woman to win three gold medals in one staging of the Olympic Games.

B1: Thompson will go much faster, says Francis

NISSAN Innovation that excites

The Gleaner

THE LEA CREDIBILITY

NISSAN Innovation that excites

www.jamaica-gleaner.com VOL. 182 NO. 198 FRIDAY, AUGUST 19, 2016 KINGSTON, JAMAICA 64 PAGES INCLUDING GCT $60

Good as GOLD

TWO DOWN, ONE TO GO

"I have dedicated my life to the 200m. I love the 200m a lot."

Rio GOLD RUSH

COVERAGE BROUGHT TO YOU BY: FLOW JN PUMA

BOLT = GOLD

BEIJING 2008: 100M 200M 4X100

LONDON 2012: 100M 200M 4X100

RIO DE JANEIRO 2016: 100M 200M

JN Rio SCHEDULE

Women's 4x400m heats – 6:40 p.m. Jamaica

Men's 4x400m heats – 7:10 p.m. Jamaica

Women's 4x100m FINAL – 8:15 p.m. Jamaica

Men's 4x100m FINAL – 8:35 p.m. Jamaica

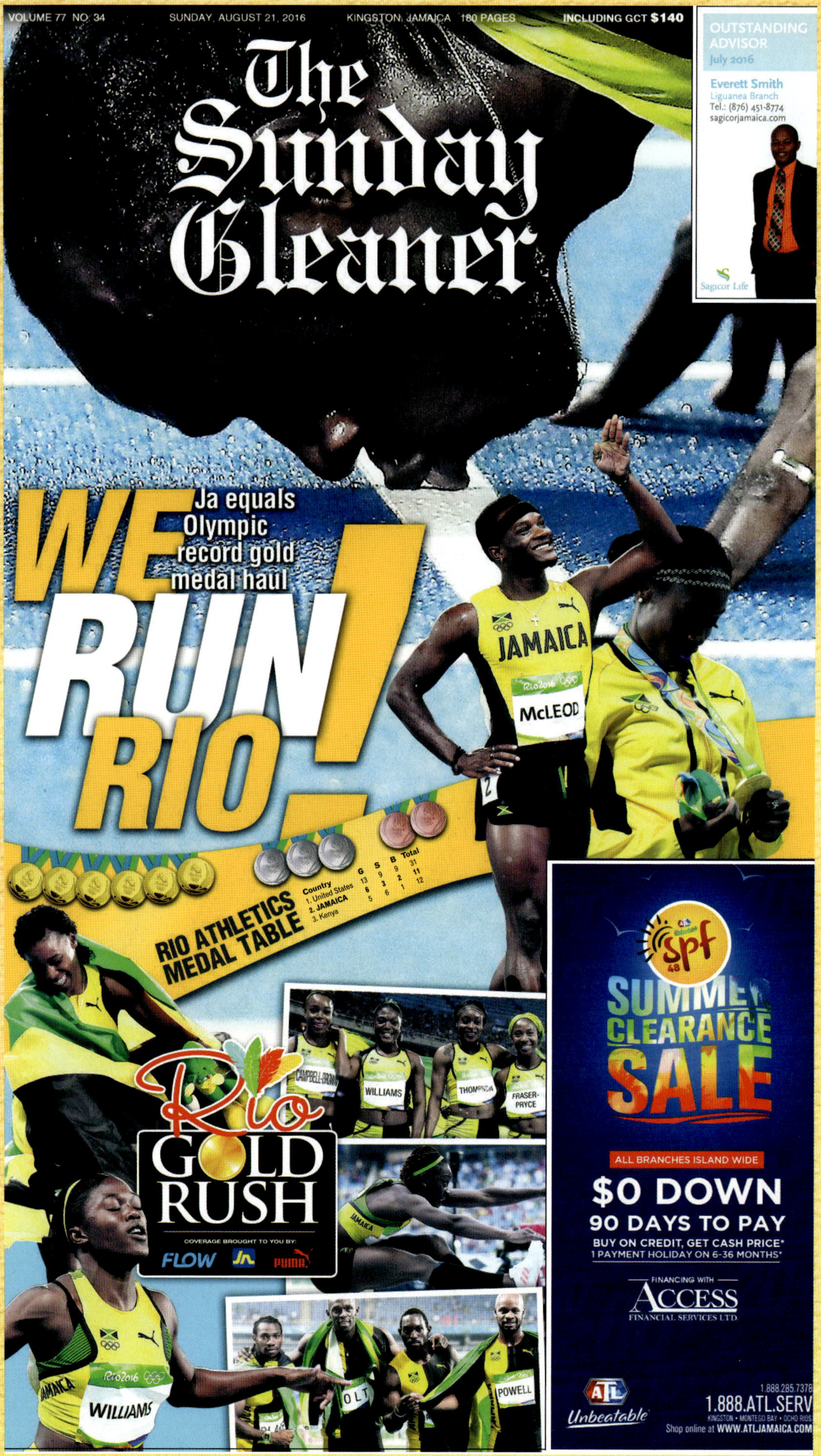

VOLUME 77 NO. 34 SUNDAY, AUGUST 21, 2016 KINGSTON, JAMAICA 180 PAGES INCLUDING GCT $140

The Sunday Gleaner

WE RUN RIO!

Ja equals Olympic record gold medal haul

RIO ATHLETICS MEDAL TABLE

Country	G	S	B	Total
1. United States	13	9	9	31
2. JAMAICA	6	3	2	11
3. Kenya	5	6	1	12

Rio GOLD RUSH
COVERAGE BROUGHT TO YOU BY: FLOW JN PUMA

Jamaica's First Female Prime Minister Bids Goodbye

The Gleaner
THE LEADER IN CREDIBILITY

www.jamaica-gleaner.com VOLUME 183 NO. 151 WEDNESDAY, JUNE 28, 2017 KINGSTON, JAMAICA 68 PAGES INCLUDING GCT $60

PORTIA'S JOURNEY

I endured it all, says retiring MP

Jovan Johnson
Staff Reporter

DECLARING SHE has "endured it all", including claims she was illiterate, Portia Simpson Miller, Jamaica's first female minister, has bid goodbye to representational politics, 40 years after her entrance as a councillor in the Kingston and St Andrew Municipal Corporation.

Yesterday, Parliament, in a joint sitting, paid tribute to the 71-year-old, who used her last address to the nation's legislature to track how she got elected to the House in 1976, her nine terms representing St Andrew South Western, her election to head the People's National Party,

PLEASE SEE **PORTIA**, A2

>> PAGE A2: Simpson Miller lauded as defender of the poor

PHOTOS BY RUDOLPH BROWN/PHOTOGRAPHER

Former Prime Minister Portia Simpson Miller walks out of Gordon House for the final time yesterday.

Inset: Simpson Miller making her final address to the nation's Parliament.

Former Prime Minister Portia Simpson Miller takes her salute in the nation's Parliament then says goodbye.

2017

First Female President of Methodist Church

THE SUNDAY GLEANER, JULY 8, 2018 | **NEWS**

New Methodist bishop to be installed today

THE JAMAICA Methodist District will see a change in its leadership today when the Reverend Christine Gooden Benguche becomes the first female president of the 229-year old church in Jamaica.

The induction service will be held at the historic Coke Methodist Church at East Parade in downtown Kingston, beginning at 4 p.m.

Gooden Benguche will take over the reins from Bishop Everald Galbraith, who headed the Jamaica Methodist District for the past nine years and who has now been appointed president of the Methodist Church in the Caribbean and the Americas.

Congregants from the 27 Methodist circuits across the island, as well as guests from other denominations and civil society, are expected to be in attendance at the induction service.

Gooden Benguche was selected to become the new head of the Methodist Church in Jamaica at the District Conference held in January this year.

Before this appointment, she served in a number of circuits both in Guyana and in Jamaica and is currently the superintendent minister for the Western St Andrew and Grateful Hill Circuits as well as the District Conference Secretary.

GOODEN BENGUCHE

Outgoing Bishop Rev'd Everald Galbraith presents Bishop Christine Marie Gooden-Benguche with the Gavel, at the induction and recognition of district president as bishop held at the Coke Methodist church on Sunday, July 8, 2018.

2018

THURSDAY OCTOBER 18, 2018 | VOL 184 . NO 249 . PAGES: 52 | KINGSTON, JAMAICA | www.jamaica-gleaner.com GCT INC. $70

The Gleaner

Salute to the Reggae Girlz: Prime Minister Andrew Holness
"This historic victory and qualification places the girls in the pantheon of the greatest sports teams of all time from Jamaica. This win symbolises the culmination of years of hard work and dedication by the team and management. I congratulate the team and management on making Jamaica proud. I call on all Jamaicans to rally behind the Reggae Girlz and give them all the support they need."

Fruits of our labour. B1

REGGAE GIRLZ SECURE HISTORIC WORLD CUP QUALIFICATION

WONDER women

Andre Lowe/Sports Editor

"IT IS an unbelievable feeling; it is a feeling of accomplishment." Those words by assistant coach Andrew Price perfectly sum up the superhuman effort that led to Jamaica's historic qualification to next year's FIFA Women's World Cup in France.

Just eight years after a lack of funding forced the suspension of the national senior women's football programme, Jamaica became the first Caribbean nation to qualify for a FIFA Women's World Cup after yesterday's intensely exciting penalty shootout win over Panama in their CONCACAF Women's Championships third-place playoff in Frisco, Texas, in the United States.

Jamaica are now the first Caribbean nation to qualify a team to both the men's and women's World Cup, following the Reggae Boyz's trip to the 1998 instalment, which, as fate would have it, also took place

PLEASE SEE **WONDER**, A3

Main Photo: *Deneisha Blackwood (14) and Nicole McClure (13) celebrate the winning penalty kick by Jamaica defender Dominique Bond-flasza (16) to defeat Panama in the third-place match of the CONCACAF Women's World Cup qualifying tournament, yesterday in Frisco, Texas.* **Bottom (from left):** *Jamaica midfielder Giselle Washington (20) and Panama midfielder Kenia Rangel (7) battle for the ball during the first half of the match; Jamaica midfielder Deneisha Blackwood (14) celebrates the goal by midfielder Khadija Shaw (11); Panama midfielder Katherine Castillo (4) and Jamaica midfielder Khadija Shaw battle for the ball.* **AP PHOTOS**

The Exchange: 'Don't invest in cryptocurrencies'. A3

JMEA
NATIONAL EXPORTERS' MONTH
OCTOBER 2018

'We A Go Thrive – Export Fi Life'. Section D

2018

Toni-Ann Tops the World

OUTSTANDING ADVISOR
November 2019
Selena Chin
Knutsford Branch
Tel.: (876) 412-5631
sagicor.com

The Sunday Gleaner

185
1834-2019

10 Days 'til CHRISTMAS

D1: 'Cat' Coore happy for Koffee, but ...

A3: Political parties prepping for March poll?

INCLUDING GCT **$150**

www.jamaica-gleaner.com VOL 185 NO 50 DECEMBER 15, 2019 KINGSTON, JAMAICA 164 PAGES

Singh to the World

AP

Miss World 2019 Toni-Ann Singh of Jamaica is congratulated by other contestants after winning the award during the 69th annual Miss World competition at the Excel centre in London, England, yesterday.

J'can beauty Toni-Ann brings home coveted international pageant title

Carlene Davis
Gleaner Writer

IT'S BEEN 26 years in the making, but on Saturday night in London, England, Toni-Ann Singh would not be denied the title of Miss World.

Singh made history, becoming Jamaica's fourth Miss World, the first since Lisa Hanna took the crown in 1993. She also joins title-holders Carole Joan Crawford, who won in 1963, and Cindy Breakspeare, the 1976 winner.

Twenty-three-year-old Singh, who hails from St Thomas, is a women's studies and psychology student at Florida State University who aspires to be a medical doctor.

Declaring that her desire is to be an inspiration to others, Singh went to social media after her victory to send a message to young women from her parish and beyond.

"To that little girl in St Thomas, Jamaica, and all the girls around the world – please believe in yourself. Please know that you are worthy and capable of achieving your dreams," she wrote.

"This crown is not mine, but yours. It's for you to truly understand that no matter where you're from and the cards you're dealt in life your dreams are valid. You have a PURPOSE."

From a field of 111 contestants, Singh, a fan favourite, had secured her spot in the final 40 after winning the talent competition with her rendition of Whitney Houston's **I Have Nothing**. She then had Jamaicans and the rest of the world on the edge of their seats with one more powerful performance of the classic during the live coronation show, which took place yesterday morning Jamaica time.

Miss World France, Ophely Mezino, was the runner-up, while Miss World India, Suman Rao, placed third.

"I am thrilled and so proud of her beyond words. She is just a special young woman and the world is hers, and I wish her every success, and I am so proud of the way she carried herself, held Jamaica's flag high, talented, humble, assertive, confident. She will make an excellent Miss World and she will do us proud," said Hanna, who is currently a member of parliament and shadow minister for foreign affairs and foreign trade.

Hanna added that it's usually a convergence of different things that would enable one to walk away with the crown, and she believes it was definitely Toni-Ann's time.

"It was Jamaica's time and I think it could not come at a better time in our country. The mood of the country needed some lifting and I really want to congratulate her family, her friends, and her mother in particular, because I know she's very close to her mother and I look forward to meeting her. I am sure myself and Cindy (Breakspeare) will have a chance to meet her when she comes back. I know Cindy is travelling so I know that she would have wanted me to say congratulations as well to her," said Hanna.

Co-franchise holder of the Miss Jamaica World Pageant, Dahlia Harris, said she was thankful to Toni-Ann for deciding to represent Jamaica at the pageant.

"Let me tell you something, kudos to Toni-Ann Singh. She was very focused, she was very determined, she knew what she needed to do to get to this point, and she made the commitment to get it done," Harris said. "There are many people to thank, but of all the people I want to say thanks to her."

Harris said it was a very difficult year for the franchise, with the death of Aston Cooke who, along with Weston Haughton, took over from Mickey Haughton-James in 2018.

"It was difficult trying to bounce back from that loss, but, you know, it's important to try to maintain the standard. It wasn't easy on us and at times, it wasn't easy on Toni-Ann either, because it's difficult getting sponsorship, and so

PLEASE SEE **WORLD**, A3

> "To that little girl in St Thomas, Jamaica, and all the girls around the world – please believe in yourself. Please know that you are worthy ... ."

TAKEN FROM PRESS ASSOCIATION

Toni-Ann Singh embraces her mother, Jahrine Bailey.

UP TO
Apply Today!

2019

MISS W

MISS WOR

The Finest of Lines

Gary 'Butch' Hendrickson

"The timing could not have been worse," she said.

"My eighty-one-year-old father had just finished a bedtime snack – a decades-long habit of his. But, as he left the kitchen to go to his bedroom, he tripped and fell flat on his forehead. This had been his home since 1970. In his 51 years of living there, not once had he fallen or even stubbed a toe. After rushing to help him, we assessed the situation. Under normal circumstances, we'd have made a beeline for the hospital. But this was the spring of 2021, and it was almost midnight. At that point we were sure of only two things: the curfew was on, and the Covid-overwhelmed hospitals were under pressure. We found ourselves staring at an unfathomable fine line between keeping him safe and attending to his injury. Would the hospital even take him? But when the haematoma on his forehead quickly grew to the size of a fist, that line vanished for us. We got him to the car and drove through the deserted streets of Kingston, straight to the hospital."

•••

In the time of the Coronavirus pandemic, we were reminded of our nation's signature brand of resilience. Rising to meet an invisible enemy's unforeseen 'attack,' we geared down and took each corner carefully. For the privileged few, the option to adapt and work from home was available. For the vast majority, however, and for one specific group, there was no such luxury for our healthcare frontline workers. At a time when we were still shell-shocked and collectively shifting our focus from living to surviving, this group showed up and performed when we needed them the most. For comforting us through their dedication to duty, I salute our frontline healthcare workers.

Don't misunderstand; that Jamaica's public health sector is beleaguered remains an incontrovertible fact. Itself at times on life support, the sector needs transparently instituted care. This, however, is what made the effort of its workers all the more outstanding: doctors, nurses, pharmacists, porters, technicians, administrative staff, and maintenance staff alike. They showed up in what was, and continues to be, arguably our darkest crisis in modern history. Again, I'm not serving up a 'Pollyannish' statement. Not every worker committed to getting into a freshly washed and ironed uniform to report for their next shift. We can't even say that most who showed up did so with a smile. Who could blame them when their own lives were at risk? In addition to the usual challenges, there was the new hurdle of ever-changing safety protocols as the pandemic continued to bob and weave. What we know with certainty, however, is that, through it all, even if the execution was at times not perfect, our healthcare workers kept those wards open. And some of these individuals, the best of the best, did spare a smile. They were the ones who looked at us and said, "You're going to be OK."

How did their effort impact us as a nation? Not to state the obvious, it literally saved Jamaican lives. As my friend whose anecdote I shared would discover, the pandemic didn't care about timing. It didn't care if you needed heart surgery, broke your leg, developed appendicitis or had a nasty fall. She still remembers the relief and gratitude she felt once her father was admitted. The team that saw him confirmed that he had, in fact,

fainted due to an underlying issue the family had been unaware of. Had the staff not attended to him that night could have ended differently. In that moment, she and her family were reminded of the one universal truth we sometimes forget when all is well. Just as the sun rises in the east and sets in the west, our health comes first. It brings to mind the maxim made famous by Marley, himself another of Jamaica's best, *He who feels it knows it.*

The real impact of the effort made by our frontline workers, however, goes deeper and continues to this day. And I'd be remiss if I didn't include those who ensure that we are safe, can eat, get to our destinations, teach our children, fill our gas tanks, enjoy electricity and running water, pay our bills, and live. If the pandemic came to plunder us of our indomitable spirit, it was our frontline brothers and sisters who pushed back and showed it that we had an endless reserve.

The threat of COVID-19, unfortunately, continues. But, thanks to our frontline workers, we know that not only will we recover from this global affliction, we will be stronger for it. We know, as those charged with our care tell us when we need it most, that we're going to be all right.

Gary 'Butch' Hendrickson is Chairman and Chief Executive Officer of Continental Baking Company Ltd.

Empowerment of Oracabessa – In Harmony With Nature

Thalia Lyn

Chris Blackwell is internationally renowned for popularizing Bob Marley, but the 52 acre Golden Eye property which he purchased in 1976 when Bob declared it too 'posh' for his taste, truly rooted Blackwell here. His love for Jamaica and community activism were formalised when the Oracabessa Foundation (renamed Golden Eye Foundation –GEF) was registered in 1995, as a catalyst for the sustainable development of the Oracabessa community.

As chair of the NCB Foundation, I've enjoyed first hand, some of the numerous successes of Blackwell, Marika Kessler and the energetic GEF Manager, Travis Grahamand and his team. Both Foundations partnered on various projects, powering up outcomes. Partnerships increase impact!

One of the best of Jamaica, the laid-back, ultra-chic Golden Eye resort, is incomparable for its rugged, sparkling coastline, massive indigenous trees and wild flora – crystalizing Blackwell's commitment to protect and care for the people and environs of Oracabessa. He established Oracabessa Foundation as the community resource arm of Golden Eye resort and successfully implemented his two main focuses: improving the well-being and livelihood of the people and preserving our Planet, utilising the 'blue economy' model in Oracabessa Bay.

PEOPLE – the Best of Jamaica

Training for GE staff and communityis ongoing, and Travis ramped it up during COVID-19.

The Jacks River Skills Training Centre (2009) in partnership with HEART/NSTA – led to over 900 people being trained in general construction, housekeeping, hospitality services and agriculture, with on-line training during the pandemic.

Two Wheels ONE LOVE BMX (2012) was the first in the Caribbean, teaching cycle-riding skills, discipline, responsibility and teamwork to local youths. The track is in a picturesque location, but formidable, a joyful challenge for young Jamaicans who love sport.

Supporting Local Growing Together (2020) provided alternative livelihood during COVID-19. It was a month-long training programme, with GEF providing supplies and technical support. Ten farms were developed. I have purchased farm-fresh broccoli and unblemished tomatoes from Ivan 'Ron' Reid, one of the 'graduates' who works in landscaping at Golden Eye. During COVID he leased land and farmed, and raised chickens. I was thrilled to meet and support him.

COMMUNITY

During the pandemic, GEF partnered with Island Grill to serve hot meals to healthcare workers, in a show of care and gratitude. GEF, NCB Foundation, World Bank, Diplomatic Pisces friends and JHTA distributed over 2,500 masks in Oracabessa, in a Stay Safe effort. Care packages were delivered in partnership with the PSOJ, Global Environment Fund, Island Grill and GE homeowners. To alleviate the difficulty of virtual classes,

NCB Foundation provided laptops to Oracabessa High and Primary schools, an effort initiated by GEF, and also granted GEF's "wish" for tablets for basic school principals, through NCB Foundation's 'Grant a Wish' Programme. GEF's Tablets 4 You digital initiative was kick-started with a donation of 30 tablets from NCB Foundation – goal: 500. Inauguration of coding classes at Oracabessa High being launched by Travis and a GE repeat guest was supported by NCB Foundation with two specialised laptops. My favourite is Christmas in Oracabessa, with locally made street banners, a store front competition and the landmark 'Big Tree' transformed into a Christmas tree. Travis entreated JPS to trim the branches and install lights, a joy to witness community collaboration!

PLANET

Fish Sanctuary (2010) – Partnership with the local Oracabessa Fishers Association increased fish size and population, enhanced the health of reefs and importantly, sustained livelihoods. Local fishermen are sanctuary wardens and the model has been replicated at the White River Foundation, with funding from the Global Environment Fund to develop three more. A fish warden's daughter, Alexcia Rose, is the NCB Foundation Parish AND national champion. I was NOT an influencer! She won the popular vote for her video on the fish sanctuary and will pursue a BSc in computer science. Kudos to the enterprising Alexcia!

Coral Reef Rehabilitation – ongoing with local fishermen trained as coral gardeners, with over 18,000 corals planted, and 17 more nurseries established, with funding assistance from the US Embassy. This project was featured as one of the Top Ten environment projects worldwide.

Oracabessa Sea Turtle Program – partnership with Mel 'the turtle man' has provided the safe release of over 50,000 turtles and became a tourist attraction for hotel guests. My grandkids have helped to count hatchlings over the years. The importance of data-gathering wasn't lost on our eldest grandson, who matriculated to become a data engineer!

Oracabessa Dive Center (2019) – Jamaica's first non-profit PADI-Scertified dive centre, staffed by local fishermen and assisted by funding from the German Embassy. More interest is being shown for diving lessons by locals, with James Bond Beach providing the ideal location – an awesome social enterprise.

Irish Moss Cultivation – still in its infancy stage, but could be a mariculture success and alternative livelihood – also funded by the US Embassy.

SMART Data Patrol and Remote Surveillance – European Union funding being used to implement sanctuary management programmes.

More and more programmes are being created by GEF, more partnerships being leveraged, to continue the successes resulting from Blackwell's vision to upskill and empower the folk of Oracabessa, and impact their quality of life, in harmony with nature through marine conservation. Future generations will benefit as Oracabessa becomes the most picturesque, sustainable coastal town in Jamaica, and one of the best of Jamaica.

Thalia Lyn is founder and Chief Executive Officer of Island Grill.

MONDAY JANUARY 27, 2020 | VOL 186 NO 23 PAGES: 44 | www.jamaica-gleaner.com GCT INC. $80

The Gleaner 185 1834-2019

Fans in shock as Kobe, daughter die in crash. B1

'Kick Kartel off pedestal'. A2

Cabinet to probe CMU muzzle. A3

Prison term cut for sex convict teacher. A3

Koffee Toast of Grammys

Sister Carol, Marcia Griffiths, Etana send congrats for inspiring women

Stephanie Lyew/Gleaner Writer

KOFFEE CAME in with **Rapture** and the Grammy Award for Best Reggae Album got captured.

The reggae entertainer made history in becoming the first female solo act to win the Best Reggae Album award at the 62nd staging of the Grammy Awards – a launching pad for other emerging and seasoned women artistes.

Rastafarian reggae singer Sister Carol, who was nominated in the category for her **Lyrically Potent** album in 1997, was delighted to know that another woman was not only nominated, but this time walked away with the award.

"I am very proud to know that finally, they are recognising the feminine entity. I am looking forward to more good music from her. And I nuh con nuhbody, so I say nuff I-gratulations, Sister," Sister Carol told **The Gleaner**.

Veteran reggae singer Marcia Griffiths was also thrilled for the **Toast** trailblazer.

"I am telling you that this is one of the best things to happen for our local music. I am almost lost for words," Griffiths said.

She said that the 19-year-old's glass-ceiling smashing accomplishment would open up more opportunities for women, adding that budding artistes like Lila Ike would be inspired to follow in her footsteps.

KEEPS FIRE BURNING

Griffiths, a former member of the I Threes, the trio of backing singers for Bob Marley and the Wailers, was featured on Toots and the Maytals' **True Love** album, which took Grammy glory in 2004.

"Koffee keeps the fire burning for all of us as a Grammy Award winner and a young female."

"I was so happy with my interaction with her and the way she spoke. Oh, Lord! It made me love her more. What I love most about Koffee is her innocence. She really deserves it! It is overwhelming," Griffiths told **The Gleaner**.

Etana was also the only solo female act among the shortlist for the Best Reggae Grammy last year with her **Reggae Forever** album, the first, in two decades, since Sister Carol to be nominated. The **People Talk** singer is another member of local the music sorority who was pleased with Koffee's win.

While boarding a flight from New Zealand, where she performed at the One Love Festival, Etana quickly said, "Congratulations to Koffee and her team."

Though not integrally involved in the music industry anymore, Tami Chynn was tuned into the Grammy coverage and hailed Koffee not just for her win, but the quality of her lyrics.

"She has been such a breath of fresh air. Her flows are so unique and her writing is impeccable, and I think she deserves the win so much. I am over the moon for her.

"It's amazing to have music that I can put on blast without worrying about finding the clean version – that I can listen with my mom to the littlest of children – which makes Koffee's music cross all the barriers," Chynn said.

stephanie.lyew@gleanerjm.com

Koffee raises aloft the award for Best Reggae Album for 'Rapture' at the 62nd annual Grammy Awards at the Staples Center in Los Angeles on Sunday. **AP**

CRIME SQUAD FLOP

PM calls PNP elite units failed; boasts bigger spend on national security

Romario Scott/Gleaner Writer

IN HIS most aggressive defence of his Government's national security policies, Prime Minister Andrew Holness has asserted that his administration has a more effective long-term strategy in curbing violent crime than the Opposition People's National Party (PNP).

Speaking at a Jamaica House press briefing yesterday after a state of emergency in the Kingston Eastern Police Division was declared by Governor General Sir Patrick Allen, Holness shot back at critics of his expanding use of the security crackdown to curb violent crime.

Holness characterised the PNP's strategy of establishing special squads to battle gunmen and target the kingpins of organised crime as a failure. The Jamaica Labour Party leader later took his message to a partisan audience at the Olympic Gardens Civic Centre in his St Andrew West Central seat, charging that his political rivals were peddling a "false narrative" that his administration did not have an active plan to collar crime.

He slammed the Peter Phillips-led PNP for allowing murders to climb rapidly while it was in power from 1989 to 2007, "where every single year, the murder rate rose, not by 100 and not 200, sometime it jump by all 300".

The prime minister asked where the party's crime plan was then.

"You know what their crime plan was? Their crime plan was to form various squads. And if you map the formation of squads to the rise in police killings, you would see a correlation," Holness charged at the Jamaica Labour Party Area Council One meeting in Olympic Gardens yesterday.

"I stand here today with great

PLEASE SEE **FLOP,** A3

Jamaica Labour Party leader Andrew Holness arrives for an Area Council One meeting at the Olympic Gardens Civic Centre on Sunday. **RICARDO MAKYN/CHIEF PHOTO EDITOR**

2020

Several Women Sworn in as Parliamentarians

2020

JLP floods House with women

Erica Virtue/Senior Gleaner Writer

FOURTEEN OF 18 women fielded by the Jamaica Labour Party (JLP) in Thursday's general election won their seats, among them seven newcomers.

The number brings a new record for female representation in George William Gordon House at any time to 18, fourteen for the JLP and four for the People's National Party (PNP).

In a general election blowout not seen since 1980, when the JLP won 51 of 60 seats, Jamaicans rejected the PNP's slate of candidates, among them four constituencies that featured two-woman contests.

For the PNP, Natalie Neita, Lisa Hanna, Denise Daley, and Angela Brown Burke survived.

Newcomer Rhoda Crawford took out PNP heavyweight Peter Bunting in Manchester Central, while Krystal Lee tore down livewire Dr Dayton Campbell in St Ann North Western. The others include Senator Kerensia Morrison, Dr Michelle Charles, Tova Hamilton, Tamika Davis, and Marsha Smith.

Those returning include veterans Olivia Grange and Marisa Dalrymple Philibert, Fayval Williams, Juliet Holness, Juliet Cuthbert-Flynn, Marlene Malahoo Forte, and Ann-Marie Vaz.

Thursday night's record election for women beat the 12 who were elected in 2016. That number is three times the number elected in 1962 and four times the number voted into office in 1989-93. Up to Thursday, only 40 women had previously been elected members of parliament since Independence in 1962, but it jumped to 47 after Thursday's election.

Last week, Opposition Leader Dr Peter Phillips was heavily criticised on social media for comments made in the political leadership debate about obstacles to greater upward mobility of women in partisan politics.

Phillips, during the debate with Prime Minister Andrew Holness, was criticised for suggesting that the domestic requirements of women in traditional households impacted their upward movement to the representational level.

The JLP's Rhoda Crawford rides on the shoulders of a supporter in Manchester Central on Nomination Day. **FILE**

HAMILTON

CHARLES

SMITH

Supporters of the JLP who chastised Phillips pointed to Rose Leon, who, at the formation of the party in 1944, was its first chairman. Iris Collins was elected in that groundbreaking poll to become the first woman voted into Parliament.

Only one woman has risen to ultimate political leadership in Jamaica.

Portia Simpson Miller holds the record for being the only woman prime minister, as well as for being elected nine times between 1976 and 2016.

The first woman to have been elected to the House was Iris King in 1962. She was later joined by Enid Bennett and Esme Grant.

Coming closest to Simpson Miller was the late Bennett of the JLP, who was elected seven times. Olivia Grange, 74, achieved her sixth term on Thursday after first winning in 1997.

Grange was the only woman among JLP Opposition MPs for four years until Shahine Robinson won the St Ann North Eastern by-election.

Current MP for St Ann South East, Lisa Hanna, managed a double-digit win on Thursday night, barely surviving a massive swing that saw the country turned almost fully green.

Hanna said that politics was best described as "blood sport" and that many women did not have the stomach for its rigour. She suggested that a type of political "crocodile skin" was needed to buffer the poison arrows of the "sport".

erica.virtue@gleanerjm.com

Government and opposition women senators pose at the Jamaica Conference Centre in Kingston on Tuesday, September 15, 2020. They are (from left) Natalie Campbell Rodriques, Janice Allen, Kamina Johnson Smith, Sherene Golding Campbell, Donna Scott Mottley, Sophia Fraser-Binns, Gabriela Morris, Dr Saphire Longmore.

FRIDAY SEPTEMBER 24, 2021 | VOL 187 NO 228 PAGES: 60 | www.jamaica-gleaner.com $100

The Gleaner

Herah to coach Herah? B1

Sprinter's husband in line for conditioning job as MVP split looms

HISTORY RESURRECTED

Car in 1961 Jamaica Grand Prix still racing in England today. SEE STORY ON A2

POWER SHIFT

Wemyss Gorman's rise the fulfilment of gender dream birthed in 1976

Edmond Campbell/ Senior Staff Reporter

BEVERLEY ANDERSON Manley, who played a pivotal role behind the scenes in the enlistment of the first four women into the army in 1976, has described the elevation of Commodore Antonette Wemyss Gorman to chief of defence staff of the Jamaica Defence Force (JDF) as a seismic shift in one of society's most powerful symbols of patriarchy.

At the same time, retired Rear Admiral Hardley Lewin, who saw great potential from very early in the senior officer who will take the reins of the JDF in January 2022, was blunt about her appointment. "Time come," he declared.

The Defence Board made the decision on Wednesday to appoint Wemyss Gorman to head the army after interviewing three senior officers.

Wemyss Gorman, 48, will take leadership of the army in an era in which the Holness administration has advocated increased militarisation of national security, strategically relying on states of emergency and zones of special operations to combat the epidemic of crime and violence, with murders rising 10 per cent year-on-year.

But Prime Minister Andrew Holness, who is also the minister of defence, has been buffeted by a court ruling that the detention of five men under states of emergency was unconstitutional. The Government has appealed.

When Lieutenant General Rocky Meade retires from the force in January, he would have led the army for five years. Since 1998, only one chief of defence staff, Antony Anderson, has held the post for more than five years.

Wemyss Gorman's ascendancy is the culmination of a dream that started more than four decades ago.

"I think shattering is a more appropriate word because yes, we have made many cracks since International Women's Year, which was observed in 1975," said Anderson Manley, who was the then wife of Michael Manley, prime minister of Jamaica from 1972-1980.

Discussing her instrumentality in getting women to enter the then male-only JDF, Anderson Manley said the policy change in a decade of tumult and social-justice reform occurred when the Manley administration had set up its first women's desk as part of the civil service.

This was in keeping with a mandate from the United Nations that observed International Women's Year in 1975 to heighten global awareness about discrimination against women.

Anderson Manley said one of the tasks at the time was to get

PLEASE SEE **POWER,** A2

Commodore Antonette Wemyss Gorman will take charge of the Jamaica Defence Force in January 2022. **FILE**

10 THINGS ABOUT FIRST WOMAN ARMY CHIEF

1. Married to Jonathan Wemyss-Gorman for more than 20 years.
2. She is 48, has a son, James, and is an avid gardener.
3. Studied at Britannia Royal Naval College in the UK and US Naval War College.
4. Master's degree with distinction in national security and strategic studies from The University of the West Indies.
5. First female officer to attain a flag rank (any officer who denotes presence in command at sea by flying a flag).
6. Hired as customer service representative at Cable & Wireless Jamaica in 1990 then joined the JDF in 1992 at 19.
7. Went to Knox Prep School and Knox College; grew up with her grandparents in Top Alston, Clarendon.
8. Spent approximately 15 years on board various classes of ships in the JDF Coast Guard.
9. Has been awarded the Order of Distinction (Officer Class) for her distinguished military service, the Medal of Honour For Meritorious Service, the Military Commendation Medal and the Medal of Honour For General Service for operations in the local theatre. Also received award for distinguished leadership by the United Nations Women Leadership Initiative in 2015. Promoted to her current rank of Force Executive Officer in December 2019.
10. Provides charitable service to girls through the United Nations Women Leadership Initiative.

Women cling to hem of incoming army chief

Kimone Francis/Senior Staff Reporter

WHEN COMMODORE Antonette Weymyss Gorman takes the ship's wheel of the Jamaica Defence Force (JDF) in January, she will bear the hopes of a generation of women hopeful that the new chief of defence staff (CDS) will chart a sea change in the army's gender dynamic.

Already, there is a weight of expectation from women subordinates looking on, several of whom are quietly optimistic that the history-making executive officer will right endemic wrongs that have, for years, plagued the military, including allegations of sexual assault and victimisation.

"I hope that she will give us something to keep looking forward to; let us feel like we're actually a part of the Jamaica Defence Force and cause us to be respected. I hope that she will look out for our well-being and promote us according to our capabilities," one woman soldier told **The Gleaner** on Thursday, following news of Wemyss Gorman's appointment.

"I want her to make mothers feel secure and for females not to be afraid of having children with the fear of losing their jobs."

The soldier, who spoke on condition of anonymity because she is not authorised to speak to the media, said that it is also her hope that the incoming army chief will develop and support programmes that will facilitate the transformation of "ordinary soldiers into figures of versatility".

Her colleague, who also asked not to be identified, wants the 48-year-old Wemyss-Gorman, who has served in the JDF for 29 years, to "create a much clearer or less bureaucratic pathway for both genders to be able to succeed in the force".

At the same time, she said that there is no expectation for the CDS-in-waiting, who will replace Lieutenant General Rocky Meade, to favour women in the military.

"She is the best thing to happen to the JDF, and I wholeheartedly support her at the helm. I'm optimistic about the future, and I'm happy to be serving in the force at this historic time," she said.

There are others, who have now hinged their hopes of success in the military on the senior officer's rise to the top, believing that a bright future also exists for them in the JDF.

"I am truly excited about the announcement of a future CDS. It gives me hope for my own future here. It's groundbreaking, really, and I personally have high expectations of Rear Admiral Wemyss-Gorman," another army woman said.

But Dr Maziki Thame, senior lecturer at the Institute for Gender and Development Studies at The University of the West Indies, has cautioned that Wemyss Gorman's appointment not be seen as a panacea to the age-old issues affecting the military.

"While we applaud the advancement of individual women in male-dominated structures, we have to ask whether those appointments shift norms of behaviour that favour men, violence, and inequity as well as inequality," Thame told **The Gleaner** on Thursday.

She noted that women do not always support equality, justice, or freedom

PLEASE SEE **CHIEF,** A2

Commodore Antonette Wemyss-Gorman is the first female to head the army in Jamaica and the third in the world.

Elaine Thompson's Triple Gold Feat at the Tokyo Olympics

2021

SATURDAY AUGUST 7, 2021 | VOL 187 NO 187 PAGES: 28 | www.jamaica-gleaner.com GCT INC. $100

The Gleaner

THIRD WAVE

Doctors call for more restrictions, funding to fight next round in COVID-19 battle

David Salmon and Janet Silvera/ Gleaner Writers

PRESIDENT OF the Medical Association of Jamaica, Dr Andrew Manning, believes that Jamaica is now in the midst of a third wave of the COVID-19 pandemic.

On Thursday, the country recorded 326 new cases, which is the second-highest number of cases since the 381 cases recorded on April 10 this year.

When asked if Jamaica was in the midst of a third wave, Dr Manning declared, "Yes, definitely." There has been a steady increase in the number of COVID-19 cases since the relaxation of restrictions on July 1. At that time, the country recorded a positivity rate of 8.8 per cent. That figure now stands at 29.8 per cent by August 5.

Dr Manning said that the Government should reintroduce restrictions on movement and gatherings including for the church and the entertainment industry. "The virus spreads from person to person, so the more movement you have, the more the virus is going to spread. So I think the authorities are going to have to look at tightening the curfew hours and they are going to have to revisit allowing gatherings."

The surge in COVID-19 cases has serious

PLEASE SEE **WAVE,** A2

INDEPENDENCE GIFT

Jamaica's 4x100m women's relay team in joyous celebration at the Toyko Olympic Stadium in Japan. The quartet comprising (from left) Elaine Thompson-Herah; Shelly-Ann Fraser-Pryce; Brianna Williams and Shericka Jackson won the event in a national record of 41.02.

Andre Lowe/Sports Editor

TOKYO, JAPAN:

JAMAICA WILL be looking to close out the Tokyo 2020 Olympic Games on a positive note after enjoying success in the women's 4x100m relay inside the Tokyo Olympic Stadium as the island celebrated its Independence on Friday.

The team of Briana Williams, Elaine Thompson-Herah, Shelly-Ann Fraser-Pryce and Shericka Jackson delivered Jamaica's first gold medal in the event since the Athens 2004 Games in a dominant 41.02 seconds win, the fastest time ever recorded by a Jamaican team.

It replaces the old national record of 41.07 seconds.

The result also meant that 100m and 200m champion Thompson-Herah became the first Jamaican woman to win three gold medals at a single Olympic Games, a feat that was celebrated by Fraser-Pryce and the other members of the team.

"As the senior athlete, I was just ready for the opportunity to make sure we carry the stick around and we got the national record. I mean we wanted a world record, also for us, we wanted Elaine (Thompson-Herah) to get the three gold medals because the last Olympics she missed it and now she has it, so we could not have asked for anything more. We are very grateful for the effort," said Fraser-Pryce, who was picking up her eighth medal at the Olympic Games, joining Veronica Campbell-Brown as the third most successful female athlete in Olympics history in terms of the number of medals won.

Allyson Felix currently has 10 medals ahead of the women's 4x400m relay, while Merlene Ottey retired with nine to her name.

Thompson-Herah, who was involved in a less-than-convincing opening exchange with Williams, was thrilled with the three gold championships and said that while the team was hoping to secure the 40.82 seconds world record, which is owned by the United States, they were happy for the win, the national mark and the Independence Day gift to Jamaica.

"This is surreal, but I think after the championship is over, then maybe I will really realise what I have done but I have to give God thanks and to these three ladies for giving me this third gold medal," said Thompson-Herah.

"It wasn't perfect but we managed to get the stick around, we didn't get the world record but we got a national record on Independence Day, what more could we ask for?"

FUTURE OF SPRINTS

Williams, competing in her first Olympic Games, is seen as the future of Jamaica's female sprints. She responded with fearlessness and ferocity to her introduction, eating up the stagger on her first-leg rivals to get the Jamaicans going.

"I just wanted to get out quickly, do my best, execute properly and get the stick around to Elaine. I was really excited, more than nervous and I was just looking forward to add another gold medal to the collection," said Williams, now fully initiated sporting a Fraser-Pryce and Thompson Herah-esque bright-coloured wig.

For Jackson, the sprint relay gold medal was welcome redemption for a missed opportunity in the 200m, when she failed to advance from the heat after an error in judgement.

"I'm just really grateful, we all went out there to do our best, we got a national record, we won a gold medal so it's just a great feeling to go out there and execute," said Jackson.

The gold medal did not arrive without anxiety and a few issues for the ladies.

"We were ready, we came out here, and to be honest, I'm telling you, especially with relays, you have to make sure you are confident and you aren't nervous because it's a baton and anything can happen," said Fraser-Pryce.

"We were telling each other to make sure that our hands weren't sweaty, to make sure our hands were dry, encouraged to rub our hand on the ground to make sure, don't panic, don't leave me, wait on the stick, you have to make sure you're not too nervous and you don't have any mishaps."

WANTED WORLD RECORD

Jackson shared that there were exchange issues during the warm-up, which played on her mind as she made her move ahead of the final exchange with Fraser-Pryce.

"I was really watching the marker, I didn't want to move too soon. When we were around the back, I couldn't get the pass, so I wanted to wait until she hit the marker to get going. I didn't want to run leave the baton. I really wanted us to break the world record, but it didn't happen. We got the national record, so it's a great feeling," said Jackson.

The team will be looking to add to its eight medals (4 gold, 1 silver, 3 bronze) on today's penultimate day of the Games with the women's and men's 4x400m relay finals taking place.

Stephenie-Ann McPherson, who suffered an injury during the women's 400m final, is likely to miss the women's 4x400m relay, which takes place at 9:30 p.m. (7:30 a.m. Jamaica time).

The men's final will face the starter at 9:50 p.m. (7:50 a.m.).

Elaine Thompson Herah waves to the crowd after Jamaica won gold in the women's 4x100m at the Tokyo 2020 Olympics yesterday. **PHOTOS BY GLADSTONE TAYLOR/MULTIMEDIA PHOTO EDITOR**

www.jamaica-gleaner.com VOL 82 NO 32 AUGUST 8, 2021 KINGSTON, JAMAICA 86 PAGES INCLUDING GCT $175

The Sunday Gleaner

TOKYO TALLY

JAMAICA MINES NINE MEDALS AT TOKYO 2020 OLYMPICS

4 GOLD

- Women's 100m: Elaine Thompson-Herah
- Women's 200m: Elaine Thompson-Herah
- Men's 110mH: Hansle Parchment
- Women's 4x100m (Briana Williams, Elaine Thompson-Herah, Shelly-Ann Fraser-Pryce, Shericka Jackson)

1 SILVER

- Women's 100m: Shelly-Ann Fraser-Pryce

4 BRONZE

- Women's 100m: Shericka Jackson
- Men's 110mH: Ronald Levy
- Women's 100mH: Megan Tapper
- Women's 4x400m (Roneisha McGregor, Janieve Russell, Shericka Jackson, Candice McLeod)

TOKYO 2020

THE GLEANER, TUESDAY, NOVEMBER 9, 2021 | www.jamaica-gleaner.com | NEWS

Jamaican makes history becoming first woman pastor at Baldwin episcopal church

Lester Hinds/Gleaner Writer

ALL SAINTS' Episcopal Church in Baldwin, Long Island, has appointed its first woman and woman of colour to be the new pastor.

She is Rev Maxine Barnett, a Jamaica-born, who entered the priesthood after serving more than 30 years as an educator.

The daughter of noted Jamaican constitutional attorney, Dr Lloyd Barnett, Rev Barnett was born in St Andrew and, after attending Central Branch Primary School, went on to Immaculate Conception High School and later entered St Joseph's Teachers' College. After leaving St Joseph's, Barnett taught for two years at the primary-school level before teaching at Calabar Extension High School.

She migrated to the United States in the 1980s and settled in Long Island where her family members resided.

Continuing her education, she attended Brooklyn College and later New York University, specialising in the field of early childhood education.

After spending some 30 years in the education profession, Barnett entered the seminary and became an ordained minister in September 2015. She served as first rector with the Diocese of Long Island before being tapped as the rector of All Saints' Episcopal Church in Baldwin.

Speaking about her ground-breaking experience, Barnett told

Rev Maxine Barnett **CONTRIBUTED**

The Gleaner that her installation as rector of the church was delayed for two years because of COVID. It was eventually held on October 13 and the **Baldwin Herald** newspaper said the service was filled with song, dance and gifts. According to the newspaper, a joint choir comprising members of All Saints', St David and St Jude performed at the festivities. Barnett had played a role at all three churches.

Gifts were given to the new rector by members of the congregation, priests from the diocese and members of the clergy.

"This is a formalising of my relationship with this congregation. I was called to this congregation by the people," she said of her appointment.

Barnett pointed out that, because of COVID, in-person service could not be held and technology had to be utilised to keep the congregation together. To this end, she believes that technology will play an important role in how the church is re-imagined going forward.

She told **The Gleaner** that her appointment as rector has been well received by the congregation and the community.

"There has been a lot of support, not only within the church, but the wider community. I want to see the community become more involved in the affairs of the church. I want to see more women being involved," she said.

Barnett said that, while the church does not have a school, it participates in after-school programmes by partnering with various organisations within the community.

She said that she will be seeking to attract more young people to the church and getting them more involved.

Barnett said she brings that gift as a teacher to her new position and hopes to use her past experiences to build the congregation. She plans to make herself better known within the community as she seeks to attract more congregants.

"I plan to be very active in the community as I seek to grow the church," she said.

"I believe I need to find out what it means to have a church. It is not all about in-person gathering but how to strengthen the church through the use of technology. It should become a tool to assist the church. We need to find out what people are seeking instead of telling people what they should be doing," she said.

Building up the ministry that serves the community is her top priority.

William and Kate's Royal Visit

Foreign Affairs Minister Kamina Johnson Smith (left) introduces the Duke and Duchess of Cambridge to Opposition Spokesperson Lisa Hanna and other officials after the couple's arrival at the Norman Manley International Airport in Kingston on Tuesday, March 22, 2022.

The Duke and Duchess of Cambridge greet spectators at the Trench Town football field on Tuesday, March 22, 2022. The royal couple is in Jamaica on a three-day visit.

2022

Prince William is animated as he and Kate, Duchess of Cambridge, talk with Olivia Grange (right), minister of culture, gender, entertainment and sport, and bobsled officials and personalities in Trench Town on Tuesday, March 22, 2022.

Prince William and Kate, Duchess of Cambridge, play drums with an unidentified Rastafarian at Culture Yard in Trench Town, Kingston, on Tuesday, March 22, 2022.

The Duchess of Cambridge signs the visitor book during a courtesy call on the governor-general on Tuesday, March 22, 2022.

Prince William and Catherine, the Duke and Duchess of Cambridge, engaging nurses at the Spanish Town Hospital in conversation on March 23, 2022.

Prime Minister Andrew Holness with Prince William during a courtesy call at Jamaica House on March 24, 2022.

Emancipation day parade road march took place on August 1. It started at the Ranny Williams Entertainment Centre and ended at the National Stadium. The parade had many different floats and people dressed in many different types of costumes.

A section of the crowd at the Grand Gala celebrations at the National Stadium.

Jamaica Defence Force soldiers demonstrate a helicopter rescue operation during the Grand Gala.

Prime Minister Andrew Holness makes a presentation to veteran reggae singer Derrick Morgan during the Grand Gala to mark Jamaica's 60th anniversary of Independence at the National Stadium on Saturday, August 6. Looking on is Minister of Culture Olivia Grange.

The night sky is set alight with fireworks, capping the Grand Gala at the National Stadium

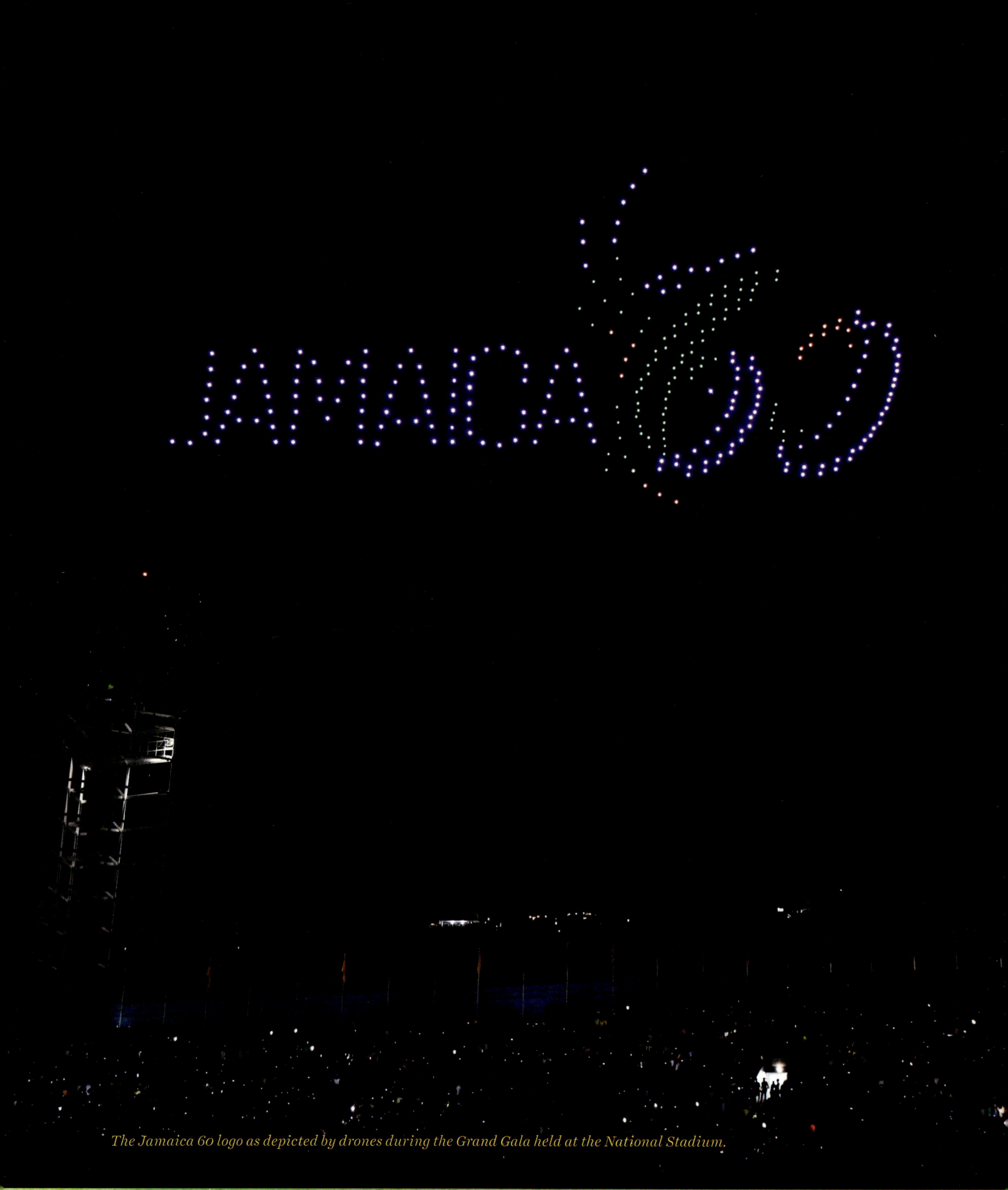

The Jamaica 60 logo as depicted by drones during the Grand Gala held at the National Stadium.